New National Curriculum Edition

INTO GEOGRAPHY

BOOK 1

Patricia Harrison   Steve Harrison   Mike Pearson

Nelson

Acknowledgements

Barratt
Linda Edmondson
James Price
Robert Rook
Revoe C.P. School, Blackpool
St. Thomas' Church of England School, Blackburn
The Ghariwallah family, Surat, India
The Patel family, Bharuch, India
The Post Office

Photographs by Aerofilms p.16, 50; Birds Eye Ltd p.46;
Blackpool Tourist Office p.48; Sally & Richard Greenhill p.60;
Steve Harrison p.14; Oxfam p.37; Elizabeth Pearson p.48; H.H.C.P.R. Ltd p.46;
Holt Studios p.45; Hutchison Library p.36; Image Bank p.39;
National Trust p.49; Network p.43; Panos Pictures p.37; Pictures Colour Library Ltd p.49;
Processors and Growers Research Organisation p.46

Cover photograph supplied by Image Bank

Illustrated by Terry Bambrook, Ray Mutimer, John Plum, Barrie Richardson,
Colin Smithson, Taurus Graphics

Original design by Barrie Richardson

Thomas Nelson and Sons Ltd
Nelson House Mayfield Road
Walton-on-Thames Surrey
KT12 5PL UK

51 York Place
Edinburgh
EH1 3JD UK

Thomas Nelson (Hong Kong) Ltd
Toppan Building 10/F
22A Westlands Road
Quarry Bay Hong Kong

Thomas Nelson Australia
102 Dodds Street
South Melbourne
Victoria 3205 Australia

Nelson Canada
1120 Birchmount Road
Scarborough Ontario
M1K 5G4 Canada

First published by E J Arnold and Son Ltd 1986
ISBN 0-560-66711-6

Fully revised second edition published by Thomas Nelson and Sons Ltd 1992
ISBN 0-17-425051-7
NPN 9 8 7 6 5 4 3 2

CONTENTS

All creatures need a place to live. These animals are lost. Can you help? Draw them in their correct homes.

Sajid and Farah live at 17, Letsby Avenue

Sally and David live at 9, Letsby Avenue.

Houses joined together in a row are called **'terraced houses'.** When only two houses are joined together they are called **'semi-detached houses'.** Do Sajid and Farah live in a terraced or a semi-detached house?

4

One step further

1 No.11 is different from the other houses in the row.
What alterations have been made to make it different?

2 Why do people make changes to their homes?
Name three changes that are often made.

3 Complete this block graph for the children in your class.

Assignment

1 Sally and David's terrace starts at No.1 Letsby Avenue.
How many houses are there in the row?

2 Sally and David have two next door neighbours.
Write down their addresses.

3 Beyond the terrace is another type of home.
What is it called?

4 Make a list of the differences between Sally's home and Sajid's home.

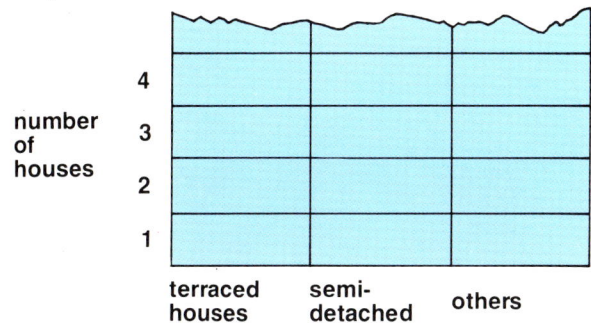

5

BUILDING MATERIALS

HOUSE 1

HOUSE 2

Why did the third pig build his house with bricks?

What materials did the other two pigs use for their houses?

Assignment A

1 Copy this chart. Fill in the names of the materials used in house 1, house 2 and your own home.

	House 1	House 2	Your Home
Roof	Tile	Slate	
Walls			
Window frames			
Windows			
Window sills			
Back door			

One step further A

1 Why are the windows made of glass?

2 Do Sally and David live in house 1 or house 2?

3 Why is Sajid not allowed to play football in his garden any more?

4 Write a story about the night Farah and Sally camped out. Here are some words to help you: howling wind, pitch black, heavy rain, footsteps, strange noises.

HOUSE A   A Cruck house

straw for thatched roof

clay infil (daub)

wooden rods (wattle)

straw

mud

willows

HOUSE B   A Victorian terraced house

slate roof

wooden window frames

brick walls

slate quarry

carpenter

brickworks

HOUSE C   A modern semi-detached house

tile roof

brick walls

window frames

tile manufacturer

brickworks

U.P.V.C. window frames

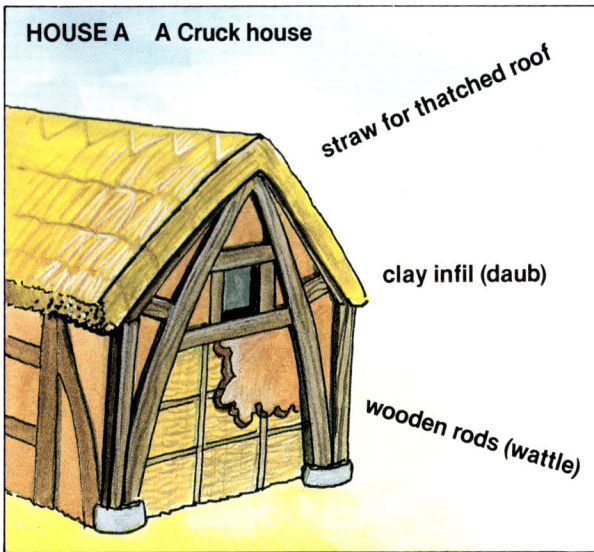

Houses built today look very different from houses built long ago. The size and shape of houses have changed. The materials used for building have also changed.

Assignment B

1   Some building materials grow as plants or are dug from the ground. We call them **Natural Materials**.

Other building materials are made in factories. We call them **Manufactured Materials**.

Here is a chart for house B.

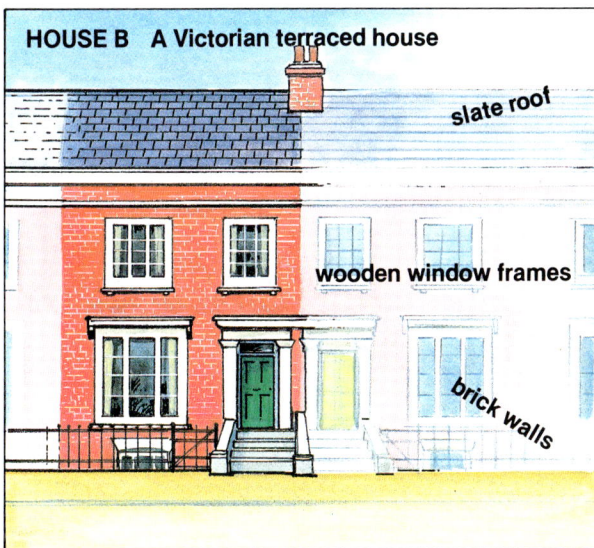

House B	Natural	Manufactured
Roof	slate	
Walls		bricks
Window frames	wood	

Now copy and complete the chart for house A and house C.

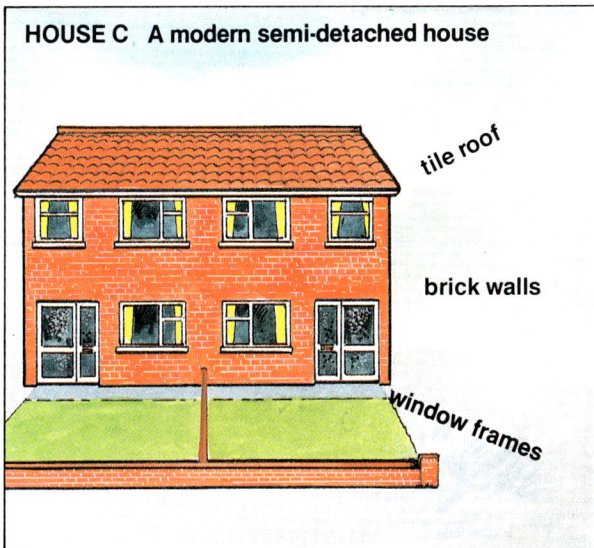

House A	Natural	Manufactured
Roof		
Walls		

House C	Natural	Manufactured
Roof		

One step further B

1   Which is the oldest house, A, B or C?

2   Draw a picture of the kind of house you think will be built in the year 2010.

LOOKING AT PLANS

David drew a Mexican on a bicycle.

Sally and David are painting the front of the new doll's house.

This is the front of Sally and David's house.

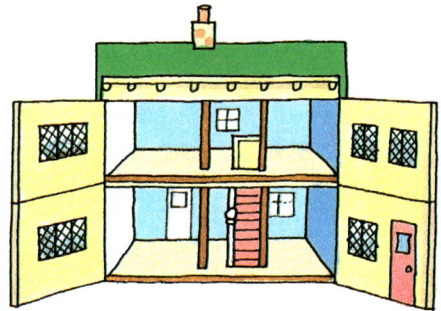

When they open the front of the doll's house it looks like this.

If we could open it like the doll's house this is what we would see.

Assignment A

1 How many rooms are there at the front of the house?

2 Name the rooms you can see.

3 How many rooms do you think there are at the back of the house. Name them.

One step further A

Pretend you are 6 cm tall. You live in a doll's house. Write a story about a day in your life. Think about the dangers. Here are some words to help you: cat, spider, big feet, vacuum cleaner.

When David takes the roof off the doll's house, he can see all the rooms on the top floor.

front

When David looks down at the doll's house from above this is what he can see. This is a **plan** of the top floor.

top floor plan

front

Now Sally removes the top floor. Only the ground floor is left.

top floor

ground floor

This is what Sally sees when she looks down. She can see all the rooms on the ground floor. This is a **plan** of the ground floor.

ground floor plan

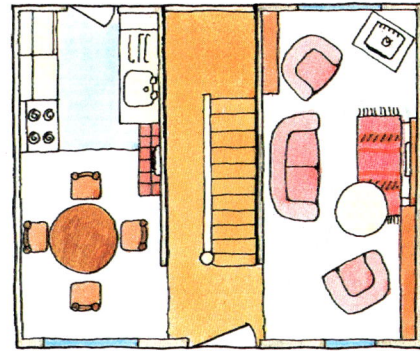

front

Assignment B

1 Which rooms are shown on the ground floor plan?

2 How many bedrooms has the doll's house?

3 Which other room is on the top floor?

4 Which room is under the bathroom?

5 Which room is over the dining room?

6 How many dolls could sleep in the doll's house?

7 Draw a plan of the ground floor and put the furniture where you would like it.

One step further B

1 Imagine you are in bed. A giant rips off the roof and looks down at you. Draw what the giant would see and write about what you would do.

2 Now draw what you would see from your bed.

3 Draw a picture of a room in your home.

4 Draw a plan of the same room.

5 Under the plan write about what you do in that room.

This is a picture of Sally and David's Living Room.

Colour key

☐ settee	🟩 lamp	☐ T.V.	☐ coffee table
☐ armchairs	☐ stereo	☐ gas fire	☐ computer

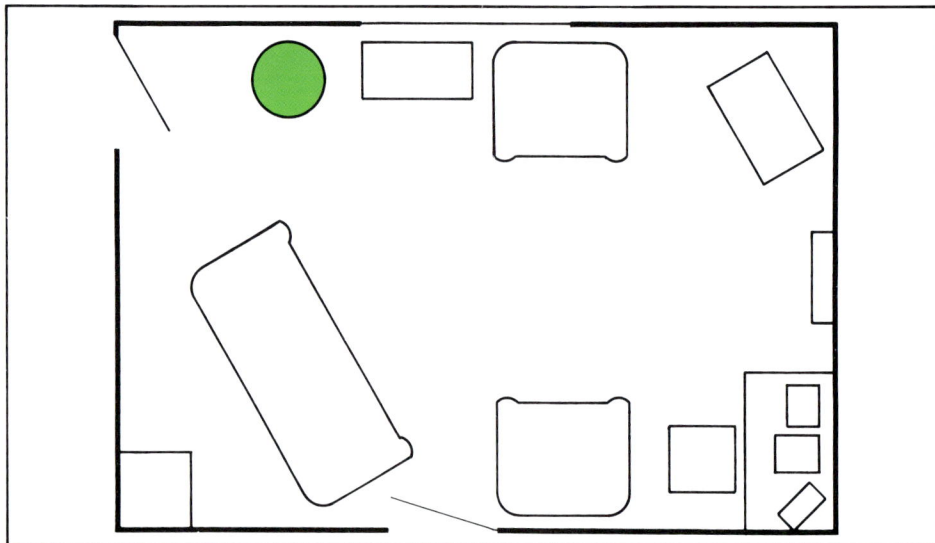

Here is a plan of their living room.

Assignment

1 Copy or trace the plan of the living room.

2 Copy the colour key.

3 Look at the picture and fill in the colour key. Use the same colours for the key that you see in the picture.

4 Now colour the plan of the living room. Use the right colours to match your colour key. One has been done for you.

5 Why do you think we need a colour key? (Clue—there are no words on your plan)

The Johnsons arrive home at different times. David always rushes home from school to watch T.V. at 4 o'clock.

Look at the chart. It shows David's movements in the living room. Using a blue crayon draw his journeys on the living room plan you have drawn in your book.

Purpose of Journey	From	To
Switch on T.V.	Hall door	T.V.
Sit down to watch T.V.	T.V.	Settee
To pick up Radio Times	Settee	Coffee Table
To switch off T.V.	Coffee Table	T.V.
To use the computer	T.V.	Computer

Copy or trace this plan of the ground floor of the Johnson's house.

When Sally arrives home she makes a number of journeys. Copy the chart below and fill in what you think is the purpose of each journey.

Purpose of Journey	From	To
	Front door	Cloakroom
	Cloakroom	Kitchen sink
	Sink	Fridge
	Fridge	Settee
	Settee	Fire
	Fire	Telephone

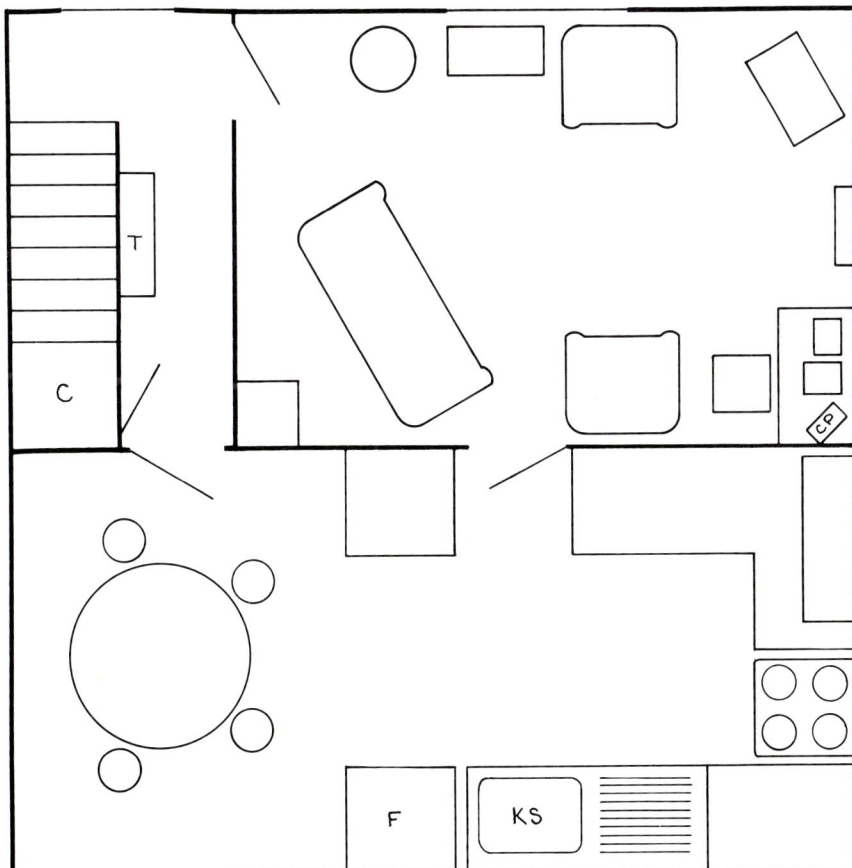

c cloakroom   CP computer
F Fridge   KS Kitchen Sink
T Telephone

One step further

1 When mum and dad arrive home there are many jobs to be done. Draw journey charts for Mr and Mrs Johnson.

Put 6 journeys in each chart.

2 Using a green crayon for Mrs Johnson and a purple crayon for Mr Johnson draw their journeys on the plan.

3 Your plan now shows the journeys of Mr and Mrs Johnson, and Sally. Which is the busiest room, the kitchen, the living room or the hallway?

With a red crayon draw Sally's journeys on your plan of the ground floor.

THE STREET

Look at the picture of Snags St.

Assignment A

1 Copy and complete the pictogram. The animal line has been done for you. There are three animals in the picture so we draw 3 animal symbols in the pictogram.

	1	2	3	4	5	6	7	8	9
animals	🐾	🐾	🐾						
children									
men									
women									
cars									
bikes									
lorries									
buses									

Now using your pictogram, answer in sentences:

2 How many more children are there than men?

3 How many adults are there altogether?

4 How many more women than men are there?

5 How many more buses would be needed to equal the number of cars?

One step further A

If you look carefully at the picture you will see that some people are in danger.

1 List the accidents that might happen.

2 What should not be happening in the street?

3 Write about what will happen next.

4 Draw a picture of the street one minute later.

5 How can the street be made safer?

12

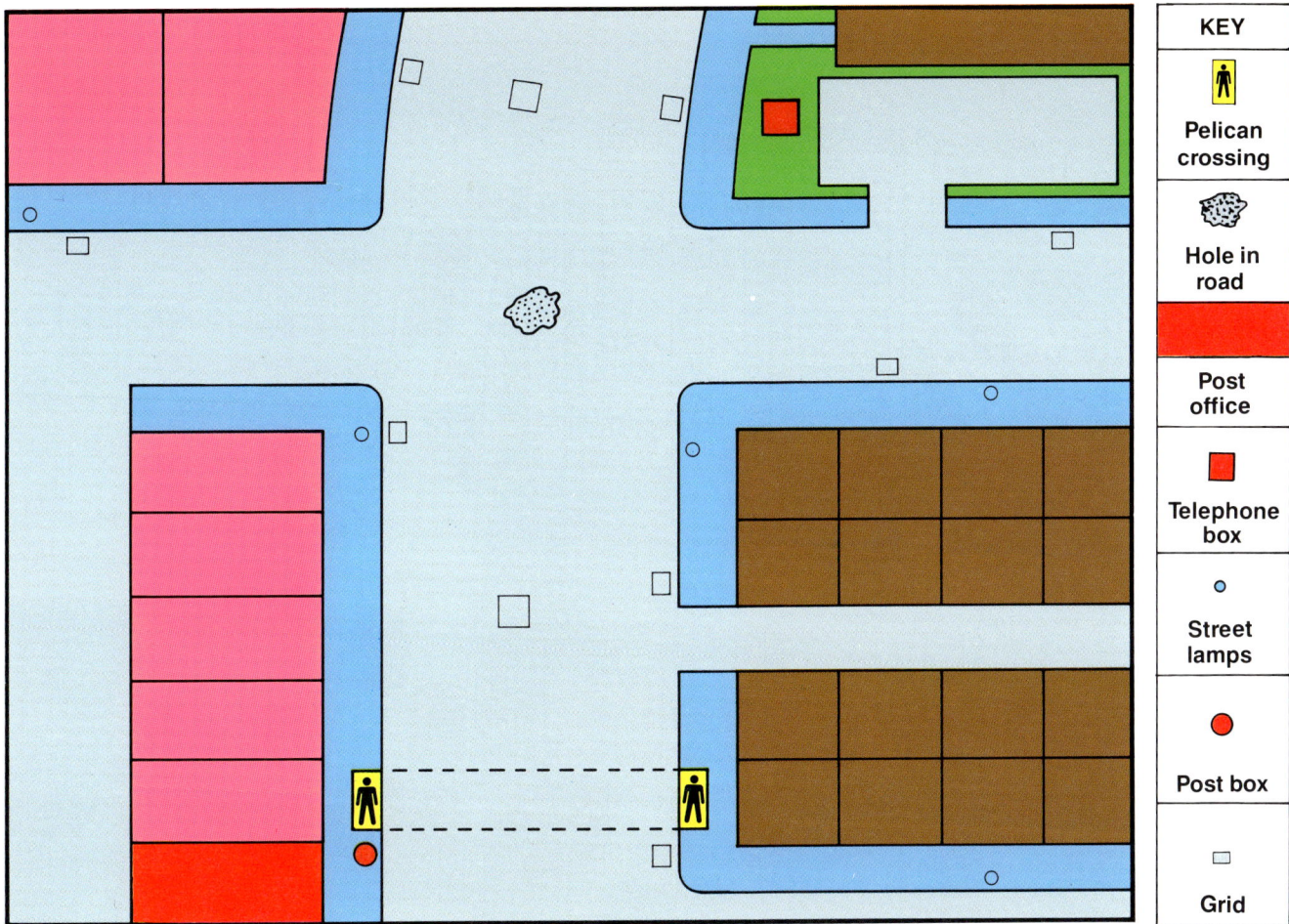

KEY

🔆	Pelican crossing
✺	Hole in road
🟥	Post office
🟥	Telephone box
⦿	Street lamps
🔴	Post box
▫	Grid

Assignment B

Make a list of what appears in the picture that is not on the plan.

Copy this chart. Look at the picture and the plan. How many of each object can you see? Fill in the chart.

STREET FURNITURE		
Telephone box	Street name plate	
Grid	Drainpipe	
Post box	Road sign	
Pelican crossing	Litter bin	
Street lamp	Bus stop	

One step further B

1 Make a copy of the street furniture chart. Complete the chart for your own street or a street near to school.

2 Are there any pieces of street furniture in your street that are not on the chart?

3 Evidence can be brought into school. Make rubbings of your street furniture.

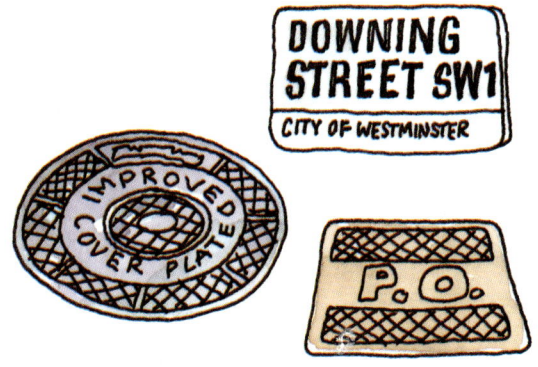

This is a picture Farah drew of her neighbourhood.

As part of their local studies work the class look at the neighbourhood from the school roof. This picture shows what they see when they look towards their homes.

They can see the terraced houses where Sally and David live, the semi-detached houses where Sajid and Farah live and the block of flats near the church. The children who could see their own homes have had their names written on the plan opposite.

This is a plan view of the neighbourhood.

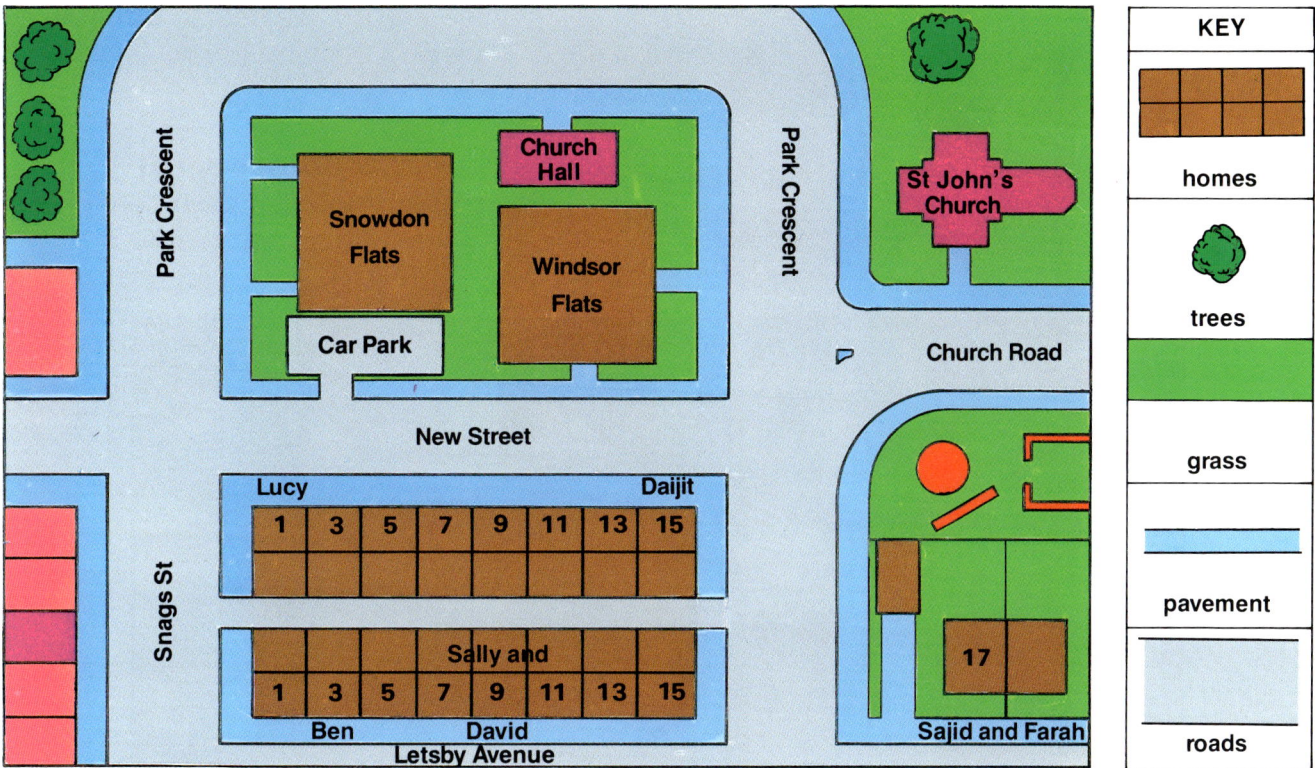

KEY

homes	
trees	
grass	
pavement	
roads	

Assignment

Some streets and buildings can be seen on both the plan and the picture. Some can only be seen on either the plan *or* the picture.

1 Complete this table

	Shown on Plan	Shown on Picture
New Street	Yes	No
Sally's house	Yes	
People		
St. John's church		
Cars		
Church hall		
Church tower		
Car park		
Sally's back yard		

2 Write down the addresses of
a) Lucy   b) Ben   c) Daljit

3 On her way to call for Lucy, Sally walks down three roads - name them.

4 Who lives furthest from the playground?

One step further

1 Follow these directions with your finger. Sajid leaves his house and turns right on Letsby Avenue.

He crosses Park Crescent and walks past Sally's house.

He turns right at the next corner.

He walks past the pelican crossing.

He crosses the alleyway that leads to the backyards.

He turns right at the next corner and stops at the first house. Who is he visiting?

2 Now make up directions for a different journey and ask a friend to follow them.

3 Tony stood on the school roof. He lives in Windsor Flats on the New street side. He could not see his home properly. On which floor does he live?

LAND USE

If we fly in a plane and look out of the window we see an **oblique view** of the land below.

This is an **oblique aerial photograph** of a town centre taken from an aeroplane.

Assignment A

1 What is the bus station also used for? How many car parks can you see?

2 How many churches can you see?

3 Which are the highest buildings – offices, shops or homes?

One step further

1 Was this photograph taken on a shopping day or on Sunday? How can you tell?

2 Why is the bus station in the centre of the town?

3 Can you see any open spaces?

The map shows the same area as the photograph. The map tells us things which the photograph does not.

Copy and complete the chart.

Building	Name of road
Bus station	
Post office	
Baths	
Museum	
Crest Hotel	

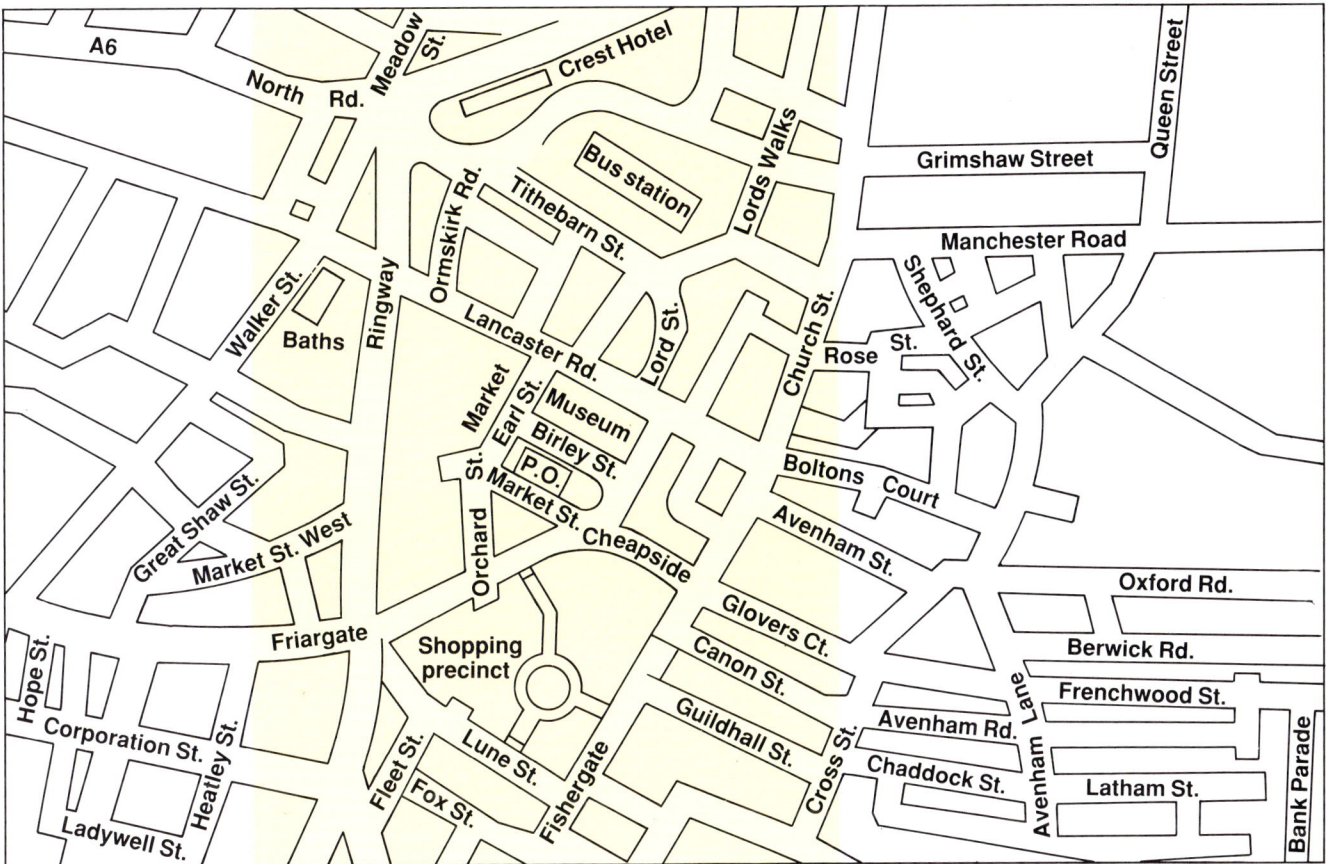

Assignment C

1 Copy and complete the chart.
What from this list can be seen only on the photo, only on the map, on both?

trees	buses	street names
people	height	building use
weather	parking	house numbers

Photo	Map	Both

2 Copy and complete the chart.
List examples of land use under the four headings.

Land use			
Shops	Offices	Worship	Leisure

Farah's classmates are practising giving each other directions. They already know their left and right. Now they are learning about **turns**.

Four directions are used:

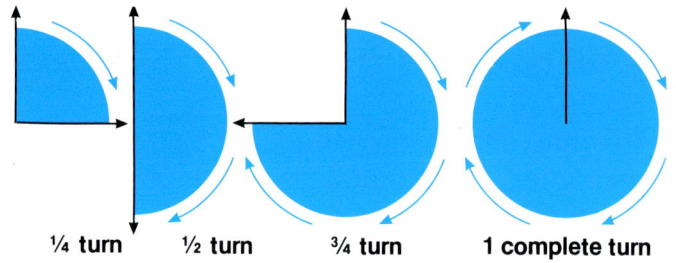

¼ turn   ½ turn   ¾ turn   1 complete turn

Here is a plan view of the children in the playground.

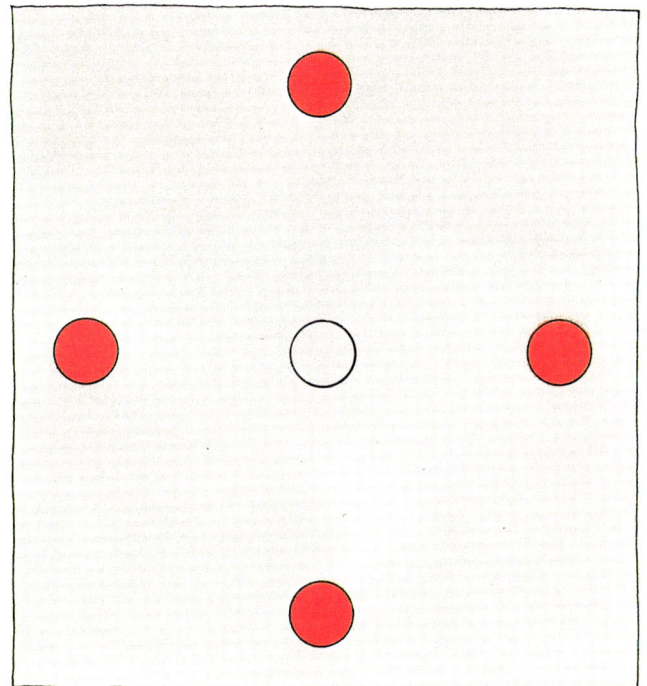

Assignment A

Farah always turns to the right. She is told who to face next. Complete the chart which shows her turns.

Start	Stop	Turn
Amita	Daljit	¼ turn
Daljit	Lucy	
Lucy	Ben	
Ben	Ben	
Ben	Amita	

One step further A

Now Farah's task is changed. She is told how much to turn and whether left or right. Complete the chart which shows where she stops.

Start	Turn	Stop
Ben	Right ¼	Lucy
Daljit	Right ½	
Amita	Left ¾	
Lucy	Left ½	
Amita	Right ¾	

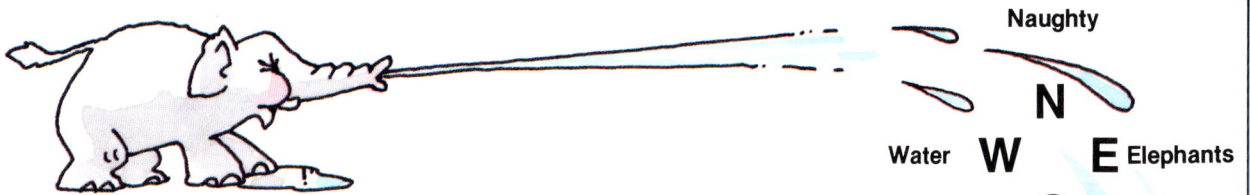
Naughty Water Elephants Squirt (compass: N W E S)

At 1 pm on a summer afternoon Farah stood with the sun behind her.

On this plan view we can see Farah's shadow. It points to the **North**.

Daljit chalked Farah's shadow on the ground with an arrow.

North / West / East / South

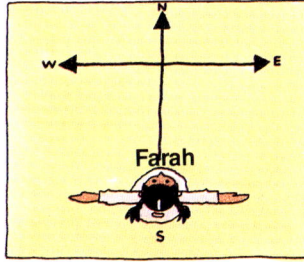
Farah

Assignment B

Answer these questions. Write in sentences.

1 In which direction is Farah's shadow pointing?

2 Where is the sun? (Behind, by the side of, in front of Farah.)

3 In which direction is Farah's right arm pointing?

4 Which arm is pointing West?

One step further B

Look at the plan of Farah and her friends on page 18. This time Farah begins by looking North at Amita. She turns right ½ a turn. She then faces **South**. Now complete the chart.

Start facing	Turn	Compass direction faced
Amita	Right ½ turn	South
Ben	Right ¼ turn	
Daljit	Left ¾ turn	
Amita	Left 1 complete turn	

Assignment C

1 Follow the directions carefully and you will arrive at a different prize each time. Always start in the square marked **X**. Write down a list of the prizes you reach.
   a) Move 1 square East then 1 square North.
   b) Move 2 squares North then 1 square West.
   c) Move 2 squares North then 1 square East then 2 squares South.

2 Now write the directions that are needed for journeys which end at the following prizes. a) Ice cream   b) Bag of gold

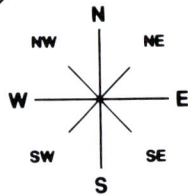

Lucy took a turn in the middle. She used a compass to find the direction of North. Amita stood to the North, Farah to the West, Daljit to the East and Ben to the South.

Lucy asked in which direction she would travel if she walked between Amita and Daljit. Amita told her that the halfway point between North and East is North-East (NE).

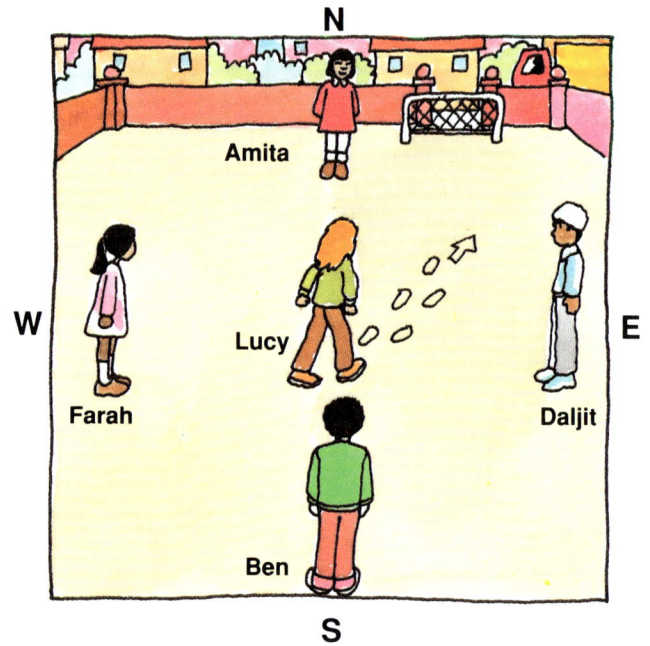

Assignment A

1 In which direction is Lucy moving if she walks:
  a) between Ben and Daljit?
  b) between Amita and Farah?
  c) between Farah and Ben?

2 Look at Daljit's puzzle. In which direction does Daljit move to travel by:
  a) bus b) car c) horse d) plane

3 Make your own 16 square grid.
  Choose one square as a starter.
  Mark it with an X.
  Write instructions for a friend.

Daljit's Puzzle

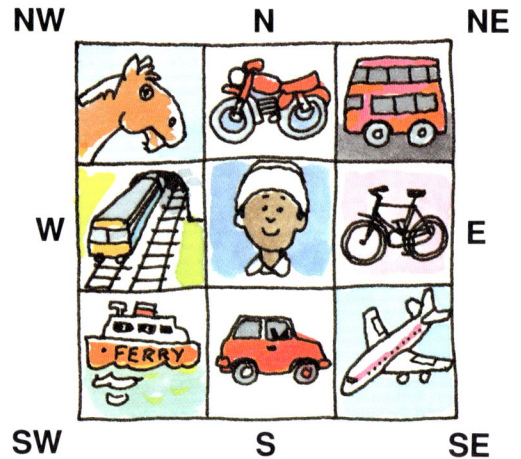

Ben and his brother are visiting a fun park. Help them plan their route around the park. Copy and complete the chart.

From	To	Direction
Ticket office	Log Flume	SE
Log Flume	Magic Castle	
Magic Castle	Helter Skelter	
Helter Skelter	Pirate Ship	
Pirate Ship	Ticket office	
Ticket office	Ghost Train	

One step further

1 Plan your own route around the fun park. Draw a chart like this one.

2 Design and make your own Theme Park Plan.
  Use 8 compass directions.
  Write questions for a friend to answer.

WEATHER

We always have to check one important thing before we go out - the weather.

I can't come out to play because it's RAINING!

Assignment A

Look at the pictures.

1 Write down what the children are doing in each picture.

2 Here are four types of weather. Which of the children's activities are taking place on a

  a) rainy day   c) sunny day
  b) windy day   d) snowy day

3 Now make a list of the games you like to play on

  a) rainy days   b) snowy days

4 Answer yes or no to each of these questions.

  a) Would you play football on a very hot sunny day?

  b) Would you swim in the sea on a hot, sunny day?

  c) Would you go sledging on a warm, sunny day?

  d) Would you go cycling on a windy day?

Remember many of the games you play depend on the right weather.

rain	wind	sun	snow

We use a symbol for the weather which everyone will understand.

Assignment B

1 Copy and complete the chart. Draw the correct symbol next to each picture.

2 We need a symbol for every type of weather. Draw what you think would be a good symbol for cloud.

3 Watch the weather forecast on T.V. tonight. What symbol is used for cloud?

activity	weather symbol
skipping	
hopscotch	
chess	
snowballing	
wind surfing	
jumping in puddles	

Farah recorded the weather every morning and every afternoon for a week. This is the record she made.

	morning	afternoon
Monday	☀	☁🌧
Tuesday	○→	☁ ○→
Wednesday	☀	○→ ☀
Thursday	☁	☁
Friday	🌧	🌧
Saturday	☁	🌧
Sunday	☀	☀

Assignment C

1 Which day was best for pegging out the washing?

2 On which day did Sajid have two indoor playtimes at school?

3 On which day did Farah go to school without a coat and arrived home wet?

One step further

Record the weather yourself for seven days. Draw a chart like the one Farah used. Don't forget to check the weather on Saturday and Sunday.

PENPALS IN THE U.S.A.

Sally and Sajid's teacher, Mrs Bond, has written to a teacher in the U.S.A. She wants her class to be penpals with an American class. The first package has arrived from the penpals. Every child has received a letter. Sajid's penpal is called Bobby. Sally's is called Jo.

This is how the package was addressed.

Mrs Bond and Class 1B
Greenhill Primary School
London Road
Newthorpe
Lancashire NN1 2BH
ENGLAND

AEROGRAMME • VIA AIR MAIL • PAR AVION

Jo wanted to know what the British children do in their spare time. Sally asked the 28 pupils in the class what they most enjoy. She drew this pie chart for Jo.

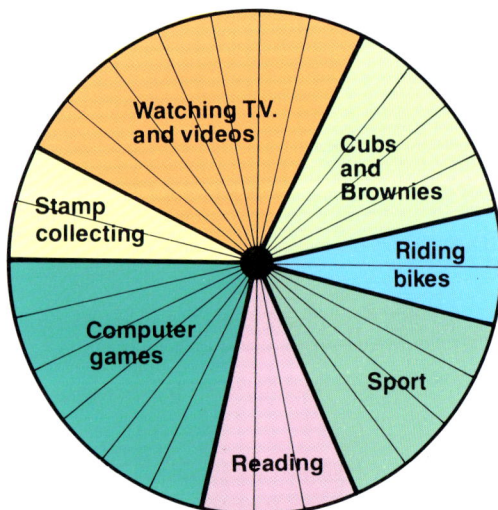

Assignment A

1 Write down the address of your own school.

2 What three things would be different if the letter had come from another school in Britain?

3 Did the letter travel by ship or by aeroplane?
How do you know?

One step further A

1 Pretend you have a penpal in the U.S.A. Write a letter. Tell your penpal all about yourself. Describe what you look like, the games you enjoy, your home, your hobbies and your friends.

2 Write six questions you would like to ask your penpal.

Assignment B

Look at the pie chart.

1 How many children watch T.V.?

2 How many play sport?

3 Which is the most popular activity?

4 Which hobby is as popular as riding bikes?

5 How do you spend your spare time?

6 Draw a pie chart to show the favourite activities for your own class.

Mrs Bond decided to send a plan of the classroom to the penpals. She drew the plan on squared paper. She put numbers along the sides of the paper and letters along the top and bottom. These squares make a **grid**.

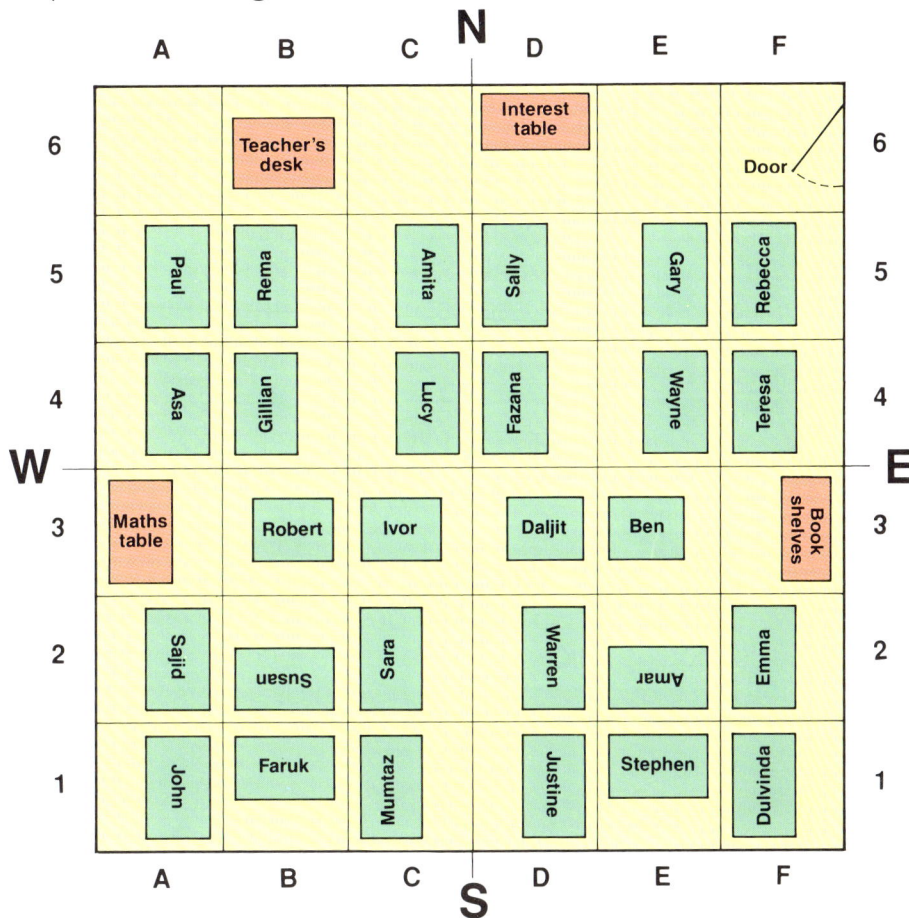

Sally is sitting in **grid square** (D,5). To find Sally put one finger on the letter D and one finger on number 5. Move your finger up the column from D and across the column from 5. Your fingers meet at **grid square** (D,5).

Assignment C

1 Amita sits opposite Sally. Who sits opposite Fazana?

2 Who sits nearest to the door?

3 Who sits in Grid Square (F,1)?

4 Who sits in Grid Square (C,3)?

5 Write down the grid squares for -
   a) Mrs Bond
   b) The bookshelves
   c) The maths table
   d) Faruk

One step further B

Remember the work on direction you did on p.18.

North, South, East and West are marked on the plan.

To reach the teacher Susan must walk North.

1 In which direction must Ben walk to reach the bookshelves?

2 In which direction does Robert move to reach the maths table?

3 Draw a plan of your classroom.

SENDING LETTERS ABROAD

Jo is Sally's second penfriend. She already writes to Ram who lives in India.
Sally decided to write letters to both her penpals. She addressed them carefully and put them in the postbox. The postman took them to the nearest main **sorting office** at Preston.

From Preston the letters went by train to two different post offices. One letter went to the foreign section at Manchester sorting office, which sends its letters to Manchester airport.
The other letter went to Reading foreign section which sends its letters to Heathrow airport.

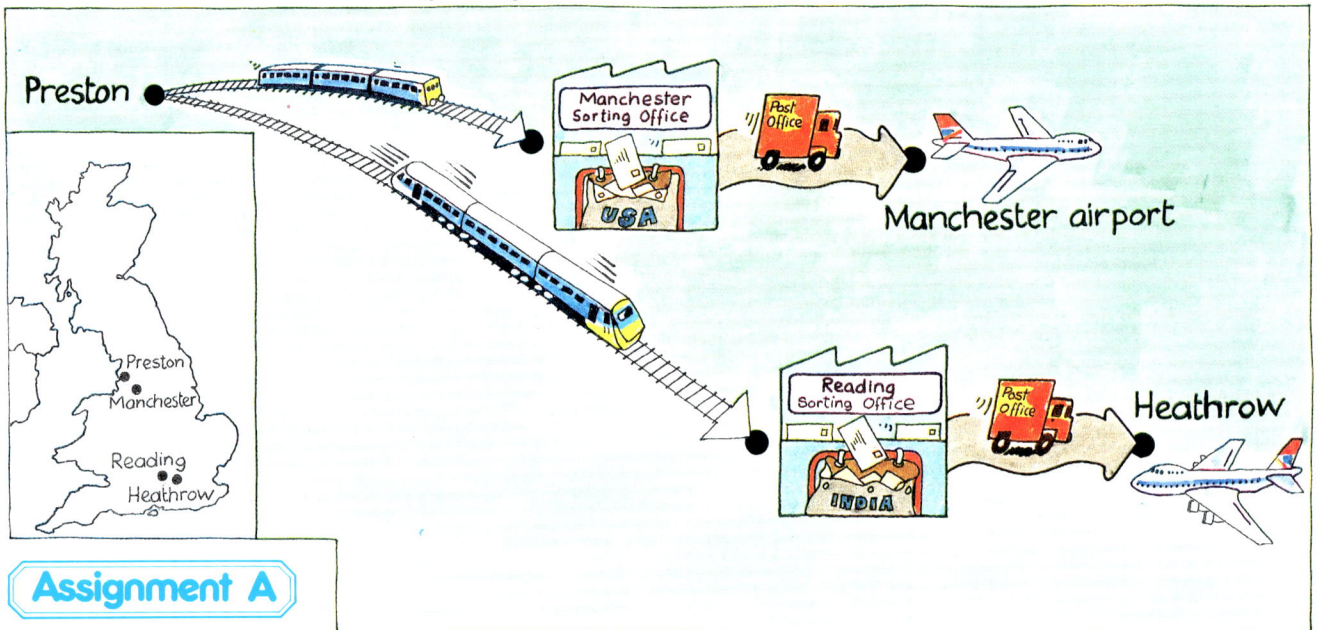

Assignment A

1 How many different journeys did each letter make from being posted to arriving at the airport.

2 Which letter travelled the furthest inside Britain?

3 Why do you think only one of the letters was sent to Manchester airport?

One step further A

Letters from different parts of Britain are sent abroad from different airports. Can you find out the journey of a letter posted in your town which is addressed to the U.S.A.?

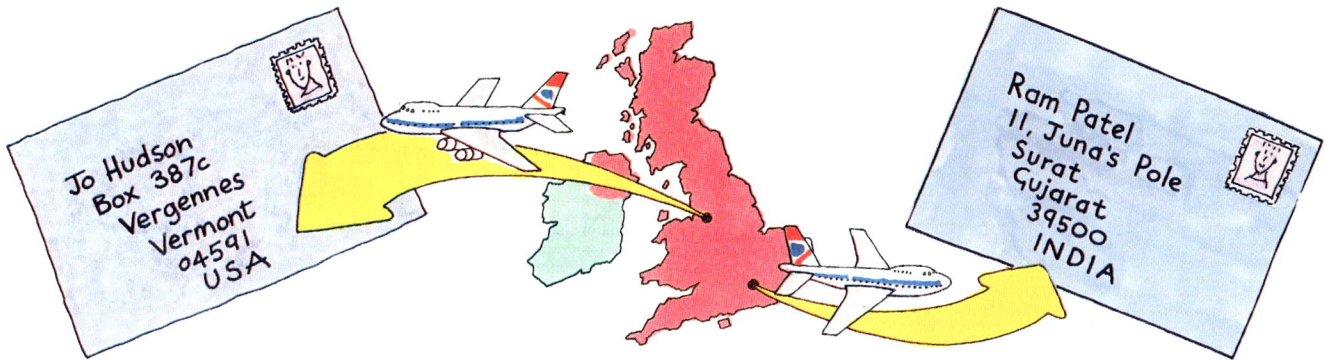

Jo's letter went from Manchester airport to New York. The letter was sorted in New York and sent to Vermont. Ram's letter flew from Heathrow airport to Bombay. It was sorted in Bombay and sent to Gujarat.

Both letters have long numbers near the bottom of the address. These are the **postcodes** (Jo calls it a zipcode). Postcodes help the post offices in the U.S.A. and India make faster deliveries.

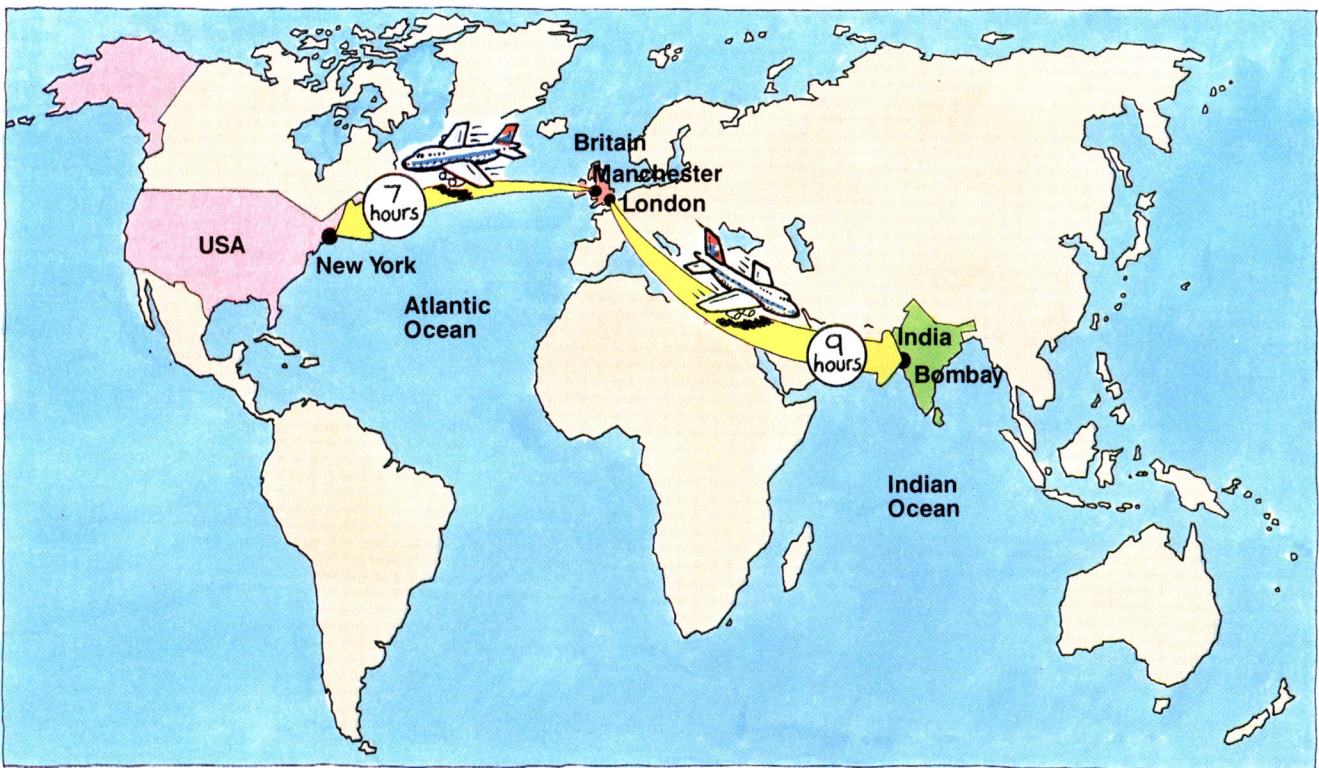

Assignment B

1 Which plane journey takes the shorter time?

2 Which is the smallest country, India, Great Britain or the U.S.A.?

One step further B

Use an atlas to help you answer these questions.

1 Which ocean does Jo's letter cross?

2 What is the capital city of the U.S.A.?

3 Is New York in the East or West of the U.S.A.?

4 What is the capital city of India?

5 Draw the national flags of India, the U.S.A., and Great Britain.

DECEMBER WEATHER IN BRITAIN

Sally and David were in the house because the weather was so bad. Sally knew that December is often wet and foggy. She wondered what the weather was like where her penpals live.

Here is the weather record Sally kept for the week from the 18th to the 24th December.

Monday	Tuesday	Wednesday	Thursday	Friday	Saturday	Sunday
◯→	☁	FOG	☁	☁	FOG	☁
wind	rain	fog	rain	rain	fog	cloud

Assignment A

1 What was the weather like on Friday?

2 How many days did it rain?

3 Draw the symbol for fog.

4 Did it rain at the weekend?

One step further A

Pretend you are Sally or David. Think carefully about the weather. Write about what you did on Friday. What did you wear? Where did you go? Begin like this: At eight o'clock I stepped out of bed and looked out of the window. 'Oh no' I thought 'not more rain'. I went to the wardrobe and .....

Assignment B

Copy and complete the chart. Look carefully at the four pictures. For each picture, say what happened, what the weather was like and what day it might have happened.

	What happened	Weather symbol	Day
A	crash	FOG	Saturday
B			
C			
D			

Sally's last day at school was Thursday the 21st of December. Here is a record of her day from midnight on Wednesday to midnight on Thursday.

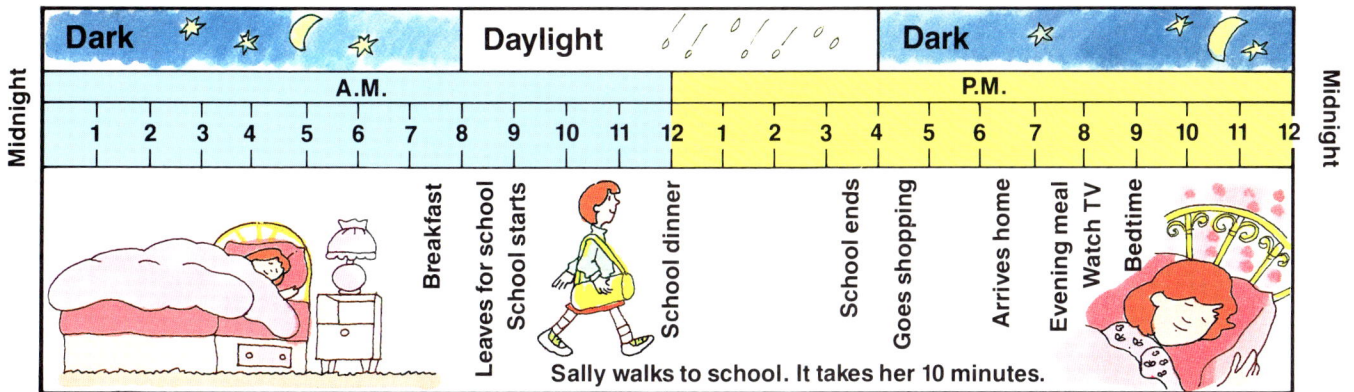

Sally walks to school. It takes her 10 minutes.

Saturday the 23rd December was a busy day for Sally. Here is her diary for the day.

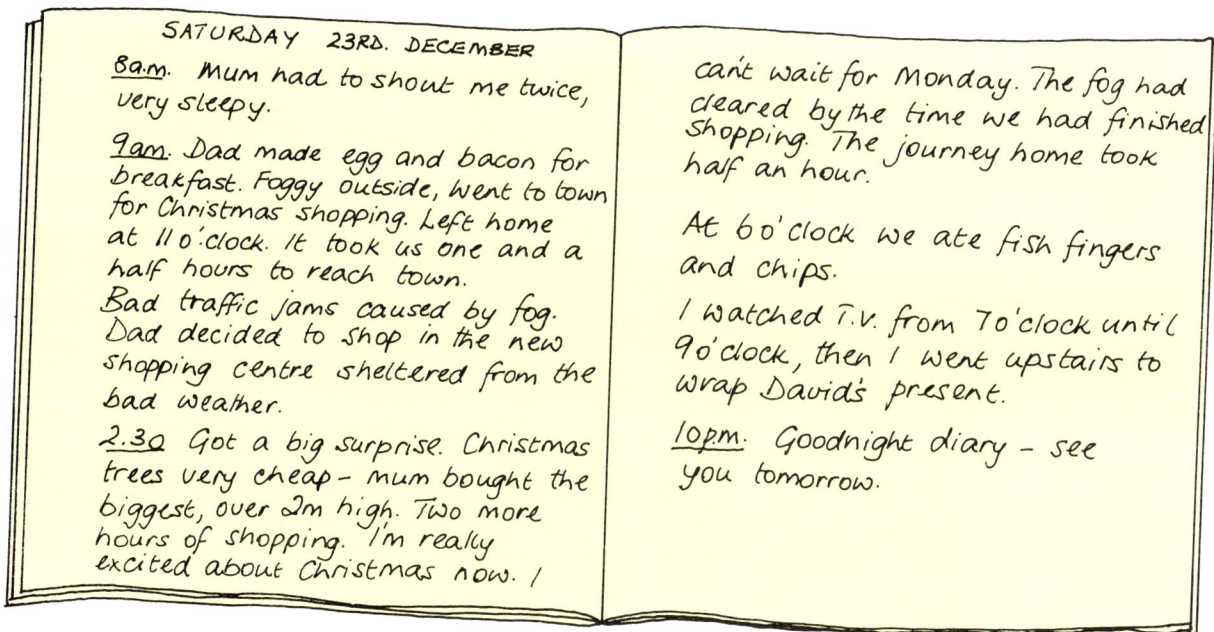

SATURDAY 23RD. DECEMBER

8a.m. Mum had to shout me twice, very sleepy.

9am. Dad made egg and bacon for breakfast. Foggy outside, went to town for Christmas shopping. Left home at 11 o'clock. It took us one and a half hours to reach town.
Bad traffic jams caused by fog. Dad decided to shop in the new shopping centre sheltered from the bad weather.

2.30 Got a big surprise. Christmas trees very cheap – mum bought the biggest, over 2m high. Two more hours of shopping. I'm really excited about Christmas now.

can't wait for Monday. The fog had cleared by the time we had finished shopping. The journey home took half an hour.

At 6 o'clock we ate fish fingers and chips.

I watched T.V. from 7 o'clock until 9 o'clock, then I went upstairs to wrap David's present.

10pm. Goodnight diary – see you tomorrow.

Assignment C

Look at Sally's record for the 21st December.

1 How many hours of daylight were there?

2 How many hours did Sally spend in bed?

3 Was it daylight when Sally went shopping?
Read Sally's diary for the 23rd December.

4 What day would be Christmas day?

5 How many hours did Sally watch T.V.?

One step further B

1 How much longer did Sally sleep on Saturday than she slept on Thursday?

2 a) How long did it take Sally to reach town on Saturday?
   b) How long did the journey home take?
   c) Why did the journey to town take so much longer?

3 Write your own diary for last Saturday.

Ram lives in a village in the part of India called Gujarat. His village is near the large city of **Surat**. Letters arrive at the village post office every morning. The villagers collect the letters themselves. Ram left the post office with Sally's letter. He then went home, sat on his charpoi and read the letter.

Sally wanted to know all about the weather in December in Gujarat.

Here is the weather record Ram kept for the week from the 18th to the 24th December.

Monday	Tuesday	Wednesday	Thursday	Friday	Saturday	Sunday
Sun	Sun	Sun	Sun	Sun	Sun	Sun

Every day in December is at least as hot as the hottest day of the year in Britain.

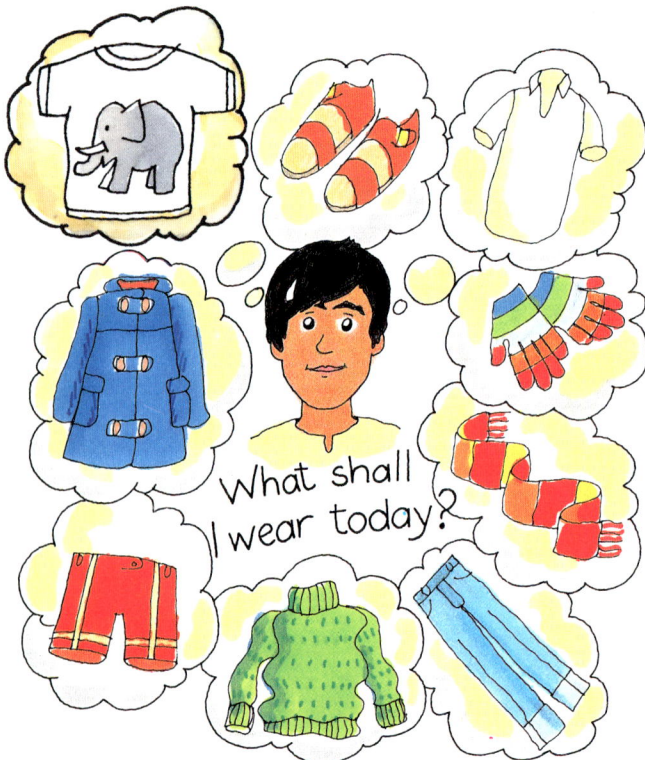

What shall I wear today?

1 What is the weather like in Gujarat in December?

2 When the weather is like this in Britain, what clothes do you wear?

1 Draw a picture of Sally. Show the clothes she would be wearing on Friday 22nd December.

2 Where would you rather be in December, India or Britain? Say why.

3 Find out where British people go on holiday in December.
   What kinds of weather do they want?

Here is a record of Ram's day from midnight to midnight on the 21st of December.

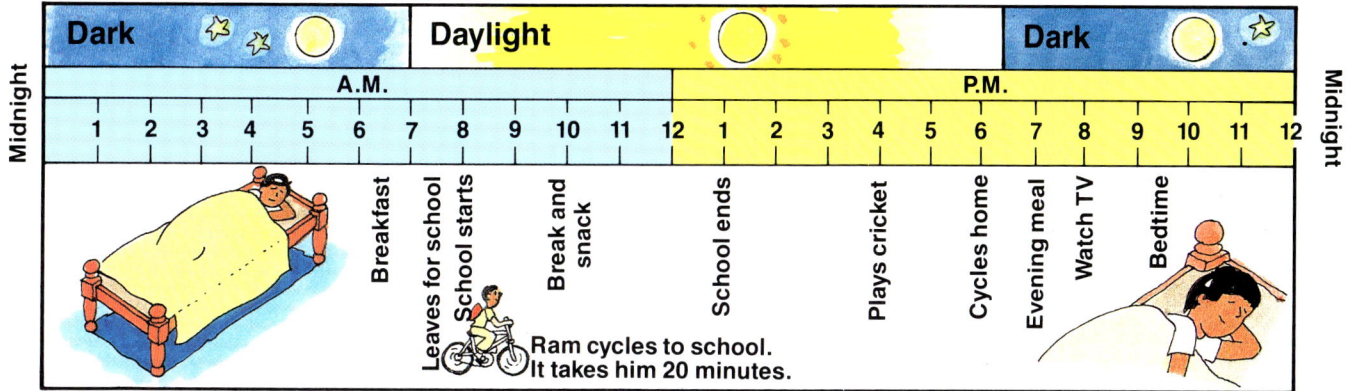

Dark	Daylight	Dark
A.M.		P.M.

Midnight · 1 2 3 4 5 6 7 8 9 10 11 12 · 1 2 3 4 5 6 7 8 9 10 11 12 · Midnight

Breakfast · Leaves for school · School starts · Break and snack · School ends · Plays cricket · Cycles home · Evening meal · Watch TV · Bedtime

Ram cycles to school. It takes him 20 minutes.

Here is Ram's diary for Saturday the 23rd December.

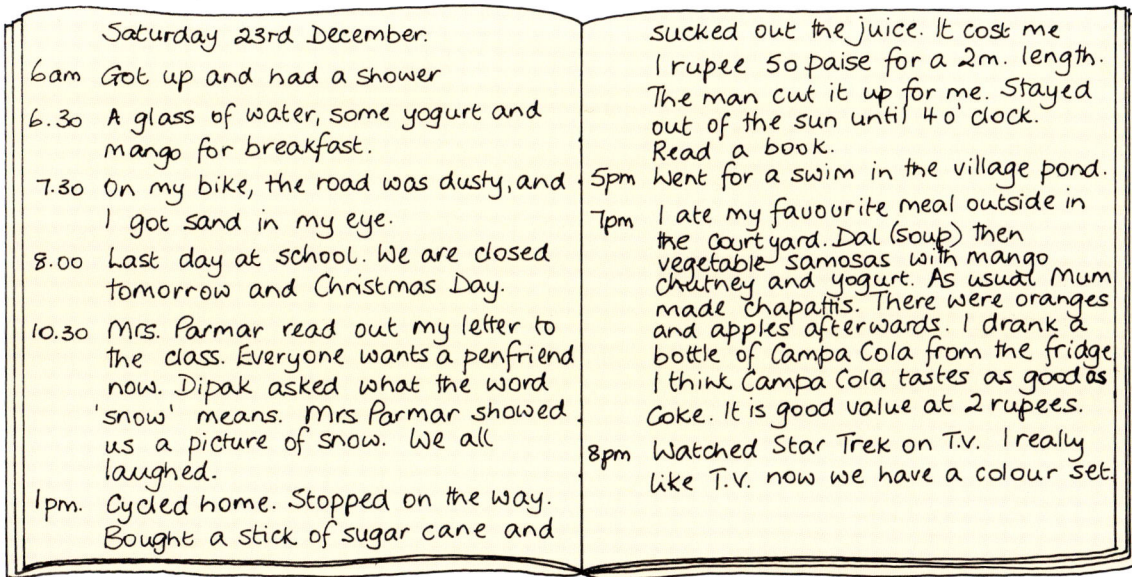

Saturday 23rd December.

6am Got up and had a shower

6.30 A glass of water, some yogurt and mango for breakfast.

7.30 On my bike, the road was dusty, and I got sand in my eye.

8.00 Last day at school. We are closed tomorrow and Christmas Day.

10.30 Mrs. Parmar read out my letter to the class. Everyone wants a penfriend now. Dipak asked what the word 'snow' means. Mrs Parmar showed us a picture of snow. We all laughed.

1pm. Cycled home. Stopped on the way. Bought a stick of sugar cane and sucked out the juice. It cost me 1 rupee 50 paise for a 2m. length. The man cut it up for me. Stayed out of the sun until 4 o'clock. Read a book.

5pm Went for a swim in the village pond.

7pm I ate my favourite meal outside in the courtyard. Dal (soup) then vegetable samosas with mango chutney and yogurt. As usual Mum made chapattis. There were oranges and apples afterwards. I drank a bottle of Campa Cola from the fridge. I think Campa Cola tastes as good as Coke. It is good value at 2 rupees.

8pm Watched Star Trek on T.V. I really like T.V. now we have a colour set.

Assignment B

Look at Ram's record for the 21st December.

1 How many hours was it light?

2 What time did school start?

3 What time did Ram go to bed?

Read Ram's diary for the 23rd December.

4 Why did Ram have to stop on his way to school?

5 Why did Ram stay out of the sun until 4 o'clock?

One step further B

1 Ram is a vegetarian; find out what this means.

2 Why do you think that Dipak has never seen snow?

3 How would you describe snow in Dipak?

4 Ram wrote to Sally about the monsoon. Can you find out what 'monsoon' means and what it is like?

5 Draw a picture of Sally eating a meal outside her home in December.

31

DECEMBER WEATHER IN VERMONT U.S.A.

Jo collects the mail from the box on the main road. He wears skis so that he can travel faster over the snow.

In her letter Sally asked Jo what the weather was like in Vermont in December. Here is the weather record Jo kept between the 18th and 24th of December.

Monday	Tuesday	Wednesday	Thursday	Friday	Saturday	Sunday
snow	snow	sun + frost	snow	snow	sun + frost	snow

Assignment A

1 What was the weather like on Tuesday?

2 On how many days did it snow?

3 Draw the symbols for snow and frost.

One step further A

1 Snow can be **fun**. Make a list of all the things you enjoy doing in the snow.

2 Write a story called "The snowman who wanted to visit India". Think about - the long journey; the ship's freezer; people staring; how to stay cool; who can help?

Here is a record of Jo's day from midnight to midnight on the 21st of December.

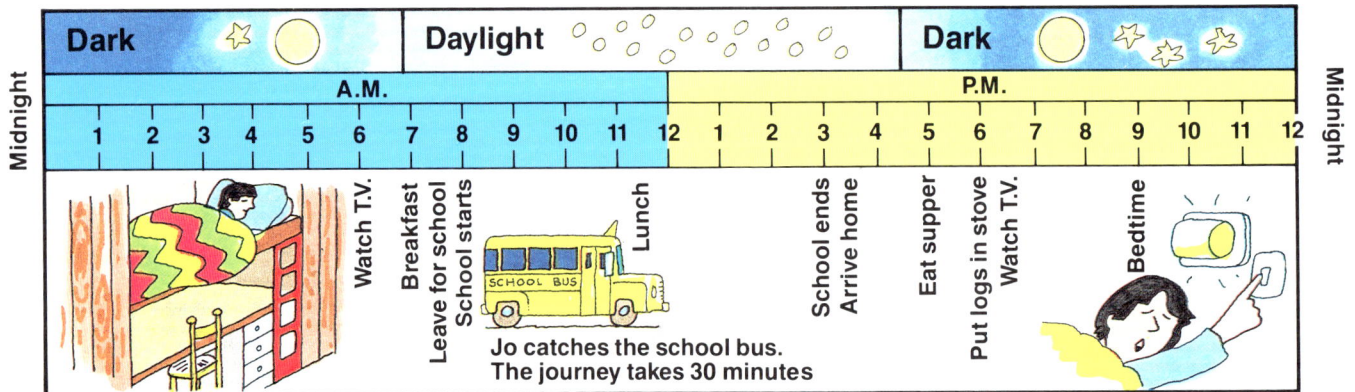

Dark — **Daylight** — **Dark**

Midnight | A.M. | P.M. | Midnight

1 2 3 4 5 6 7 8 9 10 11 12 1 2 3 4 5 6 7 8 9 10 11 12

Watch T.V. — Breakfast — Leave for school — School starts — Lunch — School ends — Arrive home — Eat supper — Put logs in stove — Watch T.V. — Bedtime

Jo catches the school bus. The journey takes 30 minutes

Assignment B

1 What does Jo call his evening meal?

2 What does Jo do before breakfast?

3 What time does school start for Jo?

4 How much earlier than your school dinner is Jo's school lunch?

5 How long does the journey home take?

32

Here is Jo's diary for Saturday the 23rd December.

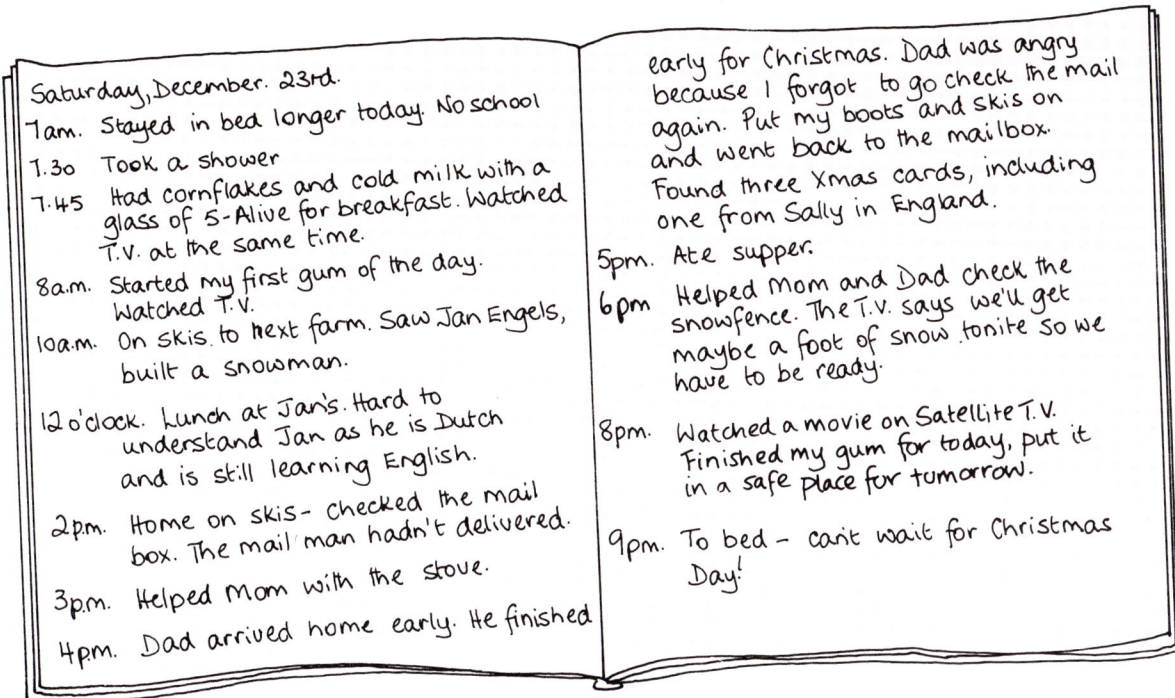

Saturday, December. 23rd.

7am. Stayed in bed longer today. No school

7.30 Took a shower

7.45 Had cornflakes and cold milk with a glass of 5-Alive for breakfast. Watched T.V. at the same time.

8a.m. Started my first gum of the day. Watched T.V.

10a.m. On skis. to next farm. Saw Jan Engels, built a snowman.

12 o'clock. Lunch at Jan's. Hard to understand Jan as he is Dutch and is still learning English.

2pm. Home on skis- checked the mail box. The mail man hadn't delivered.

3pm. Helped Mom with the stove.

4pm. Dad arrived home early. He finished early for Christmas. Dad was angry because I forgot to go check the mail again. Put my boots and skis on and went back to the mailbox. Found three Xmas cards, including one from Sally in England.

5pm. Ate supper.

6pm. Helped Mom and Dad check the snowfence. The T.V. says we'll get maybe a foot of snow tonite so we have to be ready.

8pm. Watched a movie on Satellite T.V. Finished my gum for today, put it in a safe place for tomorrow.

9pm. To bed – can't wait for Christmas Day!

Assignment C

1 Look carefully at the pictures.

Copy the chart. Say if the game shown can be played in each country in December. The first line has been done for you.

Game	Britain	India	USA
Riding bikes	yes	yes	no - too much snow
Cricket			
Skiing			
Splashing in puddles			
Outdoor Swimming			

One step further B

1 Which words does Jo use that are different to the words we use in Britain?

2 Does Jo start school earlier or later than Sally and Ram?

3 What do all three children do in the evening?

4 Who begins watching T.V. the earliest. Ram, Jo or Sally?

LIFE IN VERMONT

"Get up Jo your Dad needs help"

"Close the shutter Jo. It blew open in the night."

Jo's mother shouted from the kitchen. He dressed quickly.

Jo's dad fitted chains to the car tyres. Dad uses his 4-wheel-drive car to tow mum's car to the main road.

Dad has put up snow fences. These help stop the snow from drifting onto the drive.

The main road is clear so the school bus arrives. When the snow is very bad the school is closed.

Assignment A

1 Jo got up at 5 a.m. Why did he get up so early?

2 Is your underwear like Jo's?

3 Why does Jo need this kind of underwear?

4 Draw a picture of what the driveway would be like if there were no snow fences.

One step further A

1 Why does Jo's dad fit chains to his tyres?

2 Find out what a 4-wheel-drive car can do. How does it work?

3 Make a list of 5 cars in Britain that have 4-wheel-drive?

4 Why is Jo closing the shutter during the day?

Assignment B

Write out Jo's diary using Sally's words instead of Jo's.

Look at this list of words that Sally would use.
Mid-morning meal; really great; centre; holiday; litter; man; dustbin; motorway; café; garden; theatre; pavements; animal.

Jo uses different words.

Saturday.
Dad was on vacation. We went by car along the freeway to Boston. Gee you should have seen that place. The sidewalks were so wide and the center was real neat. Some of the streets near the theater were full of garbage. We had brunch at a diner on the freeway about 10.30.
At night we stopped at a drive-in movie. We got home about midnight.
Dad was real mad because a critter had turned the trash can over in the backyard and there was a real mess — Oh boy you should have seen that guy — he was so angry.

This is the menu at Jo's school for three days.

MENU

MONDAY	Pig in a blanket Taco chips Blueberry Muffin
TUESDAY	Fishwich on bun French Fries Fruit cobbler
WEDNESDAY	Shepherds Pie Peanut butter & honey sandwich Fresh fruit

Milk is served with all meals.

Sally sent Jo the names of her four favourite meals. Jo drew these pictures.

Assignment C

1 If Jo eats 'pig in a blanket' What will he get?
   a) A piglet in bed   b) Sausage pie
   c) A sleepy boar

2 If Jo eats 'french fries' what will he get?
   a) 2 hot Frenchmen   b) Chips

3 Is there anything on Jo's menu that you have on the menu at your school?

4 Which menu do you like best, yours or Jo's?

One step further B

1 Can you guess the names of the four meals Sally sent to Jo?

2 Now draw pictures yourself for these meals.
   a) Swiss roll
   b) Fairy cakes
   c) Hot pot
   d) Shepherds pie
   e) Cottage cheese

LIFE IN GUJARAT

Look at the picture of Ram's home.

1 How many houses can you see?

2 What is Ram's house made of?

3 How many floors has it?

4 Describe the roof.

The farmers from Ram's village grow many crops. Some products are eaten locally, some go to market and others to the factories of Surat.

Here is a grid plan of some of the crops grown on the very good soil in the Surat area.

Assignment B

Mangoes are grown in grid square (E,4). What is grown in:

1 Grid squares (A,6), (C,1), (F,3)?

2 Which one of these crops grows in Britain?

3 List the crops you can eat.

One step further A

1 Make a list of your five favourite fruits and five favourite vegetables.

2 By the side of each say whether you normally buy them a) in tins b) fresh c) frozen.

3 How do you think Ram buys them: in tins, frozen or fresh? Say why.

36

Farmers depend on the monsoon rains of summer for their crops to grow. Most years the rain arrives on time and in the right amounts. Some years little rain falls and the farmers face drought. Sometimes there is too much rain and the monsoon brings flood and disaster.

Assignment C

1 If the rains don't stop what might happen?

2 How could help reach the villagers?

3 What kind of help might they need?

4 What do you think has happened to the animals?

Assignment D

1 What materials is the house made from?

2 What has happened?

3 How deep do you think the water is?

4 What is hanging on the line? Why?

5 Make a list of all the things the family could lose.

One step further B

1 How will the women get fresh food and clean water?

2 Why is clean water important?

3 Where do you think the rest of the family is?

4 What will happen if the water keeps rising?

5 How do you think they feel?

6 How could they leave?

In Gujarat there are only two main seasons in the year – the dry season and the rainy season. It is hot all through the year.

Seasons in Gujarat, India

Rainy	Dry

In Vermont and in Britain there are four seasons.

Seasons in Vermont and Britain

	Summer

	Winter
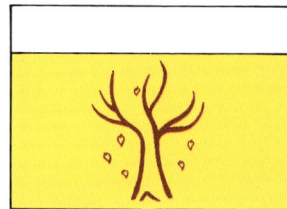	

Assignment A

Copy this chart into your book.
Think of your own symbols for summer and winter. Fill in the missing names of the seasons.

The life cycle of a Horse Chestnut Tree

Spring

Summer

Winter

Autumn (Fall)

In **spring** the leaves and blossom appear on the tree. The leaves are fully grown by **summer**.

In **autumn** the leaves and conkers fall to the ground. The branches are bare in **winter**.

Jo uses the same words as Sally for spring, summer and winter. He doesn't use the word autumn. Instead he calls it **fall**. Do you think 'fall' is a good word for describing autumn?

Can you write a poem about the seasons?

Spring

Summer

Winter

Autumn

Assignment B

Copy and complete these sentences.

1 Daffodils grow in **s**_ _ _ _ _.

The symbol for **s**_ _ _ _ _ is

2 Fruit is ripe in **a**_ _ _ _ _.

The symbol for **a**_ _ _ _ _ is

3 Skating on ice is fun in _ _ _ _ _ _.

The _ _ _ _ _ _ for _ _ _ _ _ _ is

4 The best season to sunbathe
is **s**_ _ _ _ _.

People enjoy s_ _b_ _ _ _ _ _ .

The symbol for _ _ _ _ _ _ is

Britain has four seasons; some places have only one season. In the rainforest of Brazil the weather is the same all year round. Every day the temperature is over 30°C and every afternoon it rains heavily usually with thunder and lightning. There is never a time when all the trees lose their leaves, so it is green all the year round.

LOCAL SHOPPING

Grandma Johnson asks David and Sally to go shopping for her. Sally and David are pleased because it is their mum's birthday tomorrow.

Grandma Johnson's shopping list:

```
5 stamps
1 loaf
6 oranges
4 pork chops
packet frozen peas
1 litre lemonade
newspaper
fish and chips 3 times
1 meat and potato pie.
```

Sally's secret list:

```
birthday card
box chocolates
1 film
```

David's secret list:

```
Birthday card
1 bunch of flowers
1 comic
```

Assignment A

1 Draw and complete the chart to show where David and Sally will get each item on their list:

Item	Shop
5 stamps	Post Office
1 loaf	
6 oranges	

2 What do the two road signs tell us?

3 Where will Sally and David cross the road?

One step further A

Rearrange the three shopping lists into one. Show what will be bought from each shop.

Shop	Things to buy
1 Newsagent	Birthday cards, comic, newspaper, chocolates
2	

Which items should be bought last?

KEY

Shops		Car Park	
Other services		Houses	
Empty			

This is a map of the shopping centre.

Buildings such as banks offer services for people. They are not like shops. Banks look after people's money. They also lend money.

Assignment B

1   Which buildings are not shops but provide services?

2   If you bought the empty shop, what would you sell?

3   What services does an estate agent offer?

4   How can you tell the difference between the telephone kiosk and the letter box on the map?

5   What do the double yellow lines on the side of the road mean?

One step further B

1   Copy the map. Mark in blue, the route David and Sally took to do their shopping. Start and finish at the newsagent. They can cross the road only at the zebra crossing.

2   Make a map or drawing of the local shops and services near your home. Write on it what each shop sells, and what each service provides.

SHOPPING CHANGES

This is the same shopping street as on page 40, but one year later. Have you noticed that you are looking down on the street from a different position? What other changes can you see?

Assignment A

1   The main change is that the street has been **pedestrianised**. What does this mean?

2   Complete the chart opposite by making a list of all the changes you can spot.

3   Give reasons why you think this street is better or worse than it was a year ago.

One step further A

Make a list of any changes in your local shopping street. Your parents or grandparents may know what the area looked like years ago.

CHANGES IN THE LOCAL SHOPPING AREA	
One Year Ago	Now: give the clues
One way street	No cars: sign says no entry for cars
Grocer's shop	
Empty shop	
House being pulled down	
Mr. Bones, Butcher	

Baker	2	8	Fish and Chips	
Supermarket	5	3	Fruit and vegetable shop	
Launderette	2	2	Post Office	
Chinese Takeaway	0	1	Bank	Hairdresser

KEY

- P Post box
- T Telephone
- Bench
- Clock
- Lamp

Pub 10

T P

6

Hairdresser 1

Lawn mower services 0

Bank 1

Estate Agents 3

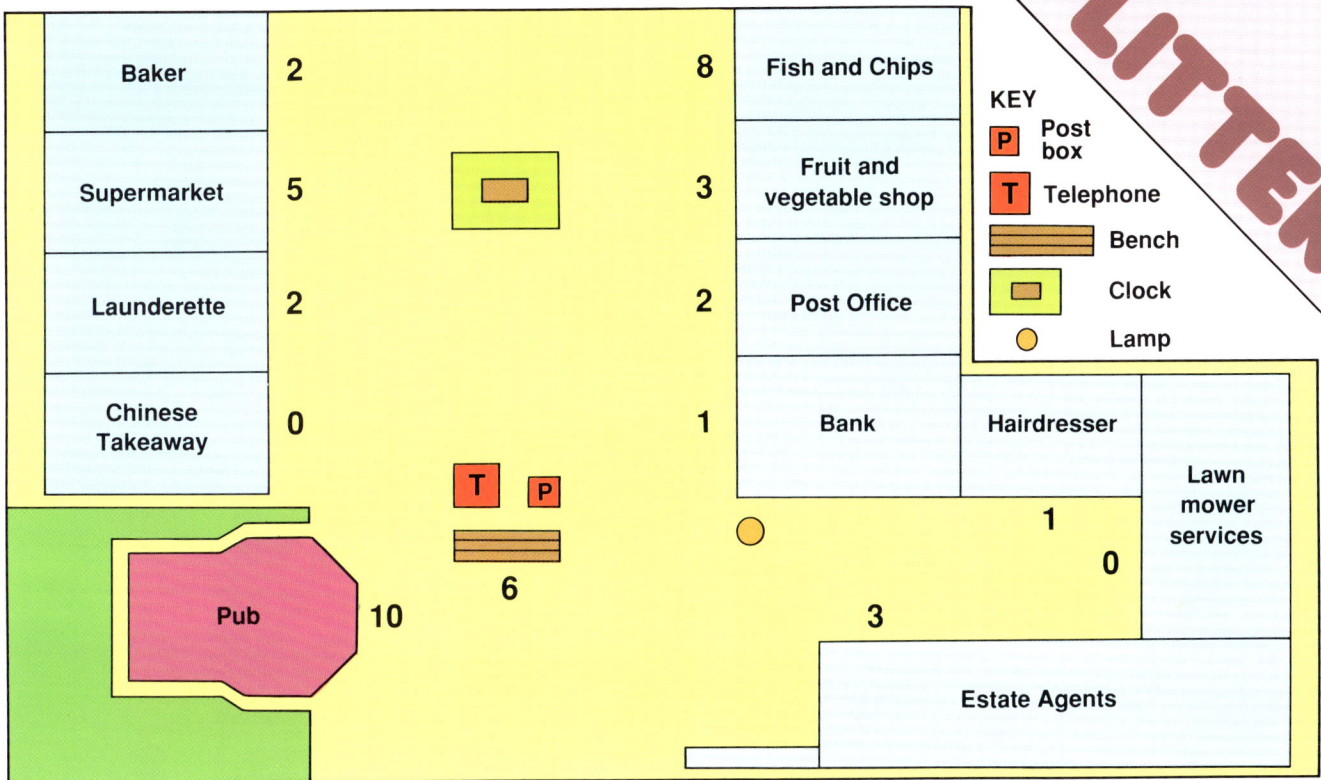

Sally and David made a litter survey outside the shops. The numbers on the plan show how many pieces of litter they found in front of each building.

Assignment B

1 Where did they find the most litter?

2 Which places had no litter?

3 The council plans to put two litter bins in this shopping area. Where should they go?

4 The law says shopkeepers must remove litter from in front of their buildings. Which have not done this?

One step further B

Visit a local shopping area.

1 Where is most litter found? Which shops sell these items?

2 Count the number of litter bins. Are there enough? Are they full? If more are needed where would you put them?

Look at the photograph.

3 Who is responsible for this litter? What could be done to stop it? Design an anti-litter poster which you would display in this shopping area.

Robert Rook is a farmer in Eastern England.

His farm is called an arable farm because he grows crops.

These are the crops grown by Robert Rook.

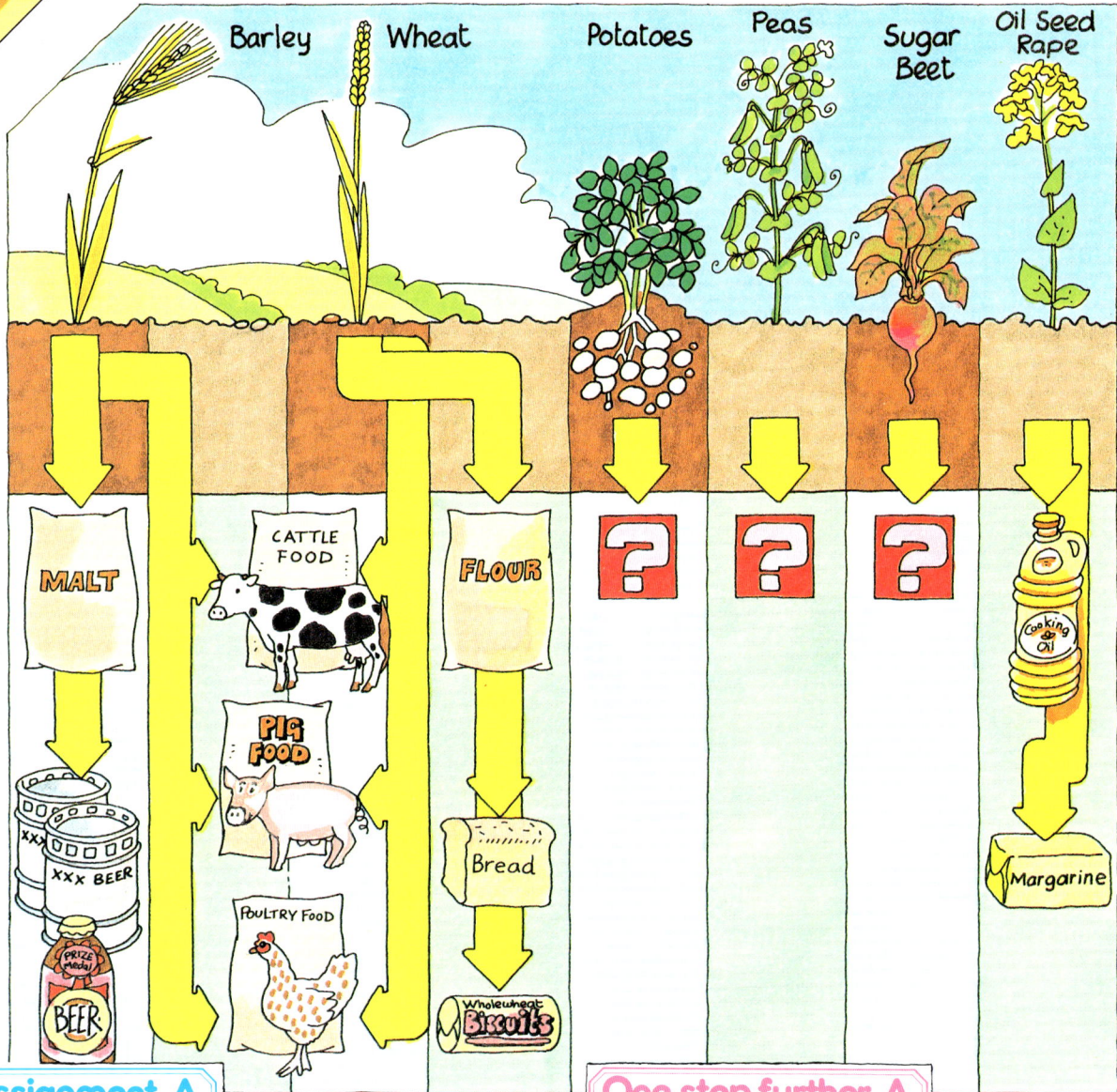

Barley   Wheat   Potatoes   Peas   Sugar Beet   Oil Seed Rape

MALT

CATTLE FOOD

FLOUR

?   ?   ?

Cooking Oil

PIG FOOD

XXX BEER

PRIZE medal BEER

POULTRY FOOD

Bread

Wholewheat Biscuits

Margarine

Assignment A

1 How many crops does Mr Rook grow?

2 Make a list of the crops and show what each is used for.

3 How can you spot the difference between wheat and barley?

4 Which crop grows tubers under the ground?

One step further A

1 Find out what crops are grown on the farms near where you live.

2 Can you find the names of two other tubers which we eat?

3 List 6 foods sold in your local greengrocers which do not grow in Britain.

Assignment B

1 Look at the round chart. Which two months are the busiest for Mr Rook?

2 When do you think Mr and Mrs Rook will have their holidays?

3 Copy the table below and fill in the months.

4 Which crop grows the fastest?

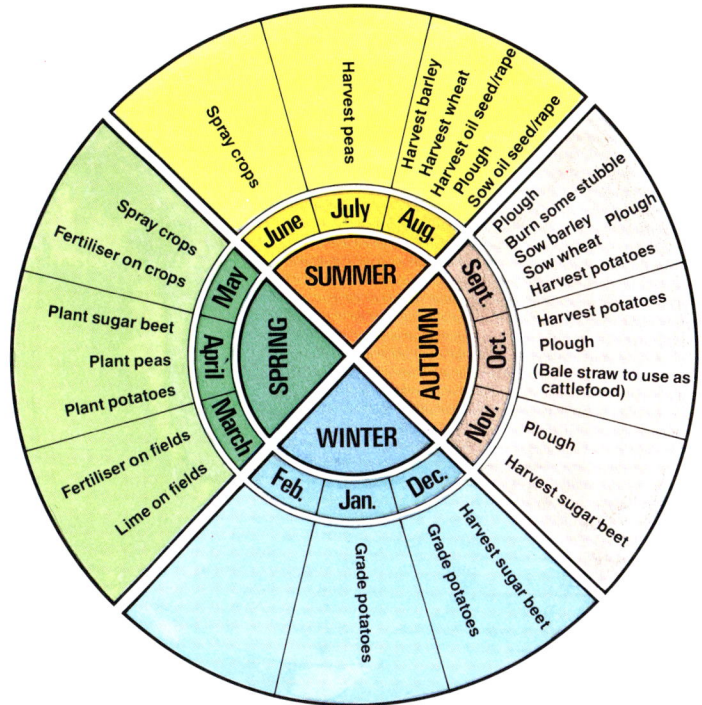

Crop	Which month planted?	Which month harvested?	How many months to grow?
Peas			
Potatoes			
Barley			
Wheat			
Sugar Beet			
Oil Seed Rape			

5 What is the farmer in the photograph doing?

6 What time of year must it be?

7 Find out why farmers do this.

One step further B

Thousands of kilometres of hedgerow have been destroyed. Sort these statements into reasons for or against removing hedgerows:

1 'Bigger fields are easier for my machines.'

2 'Without hedges the countryside looks boring.'

3 'Many birds and animals lose their homes.'

4 'It is safer. Drivers can see further.'

TWO-OCLOCK   HALF-PAST TWO

PEAS TO FREEZE

The frozen food company tells Mr. Rook what sort of peas to grow, when to plant, and when to harvest. Peas must be frozen within about 1½ hours of being picked in the field.

A pea vining (harvesting) machine.

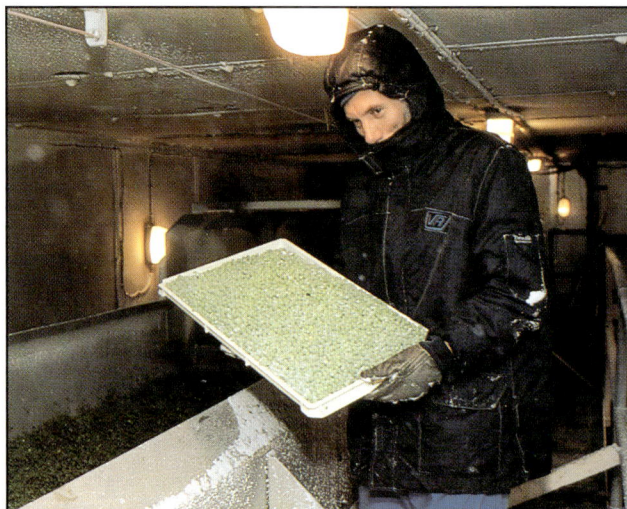

Inside a pea freezing factory.

Assignment

1 How long did it take to get the peas to the factory?

2 Why are the peas rushed to the factory?

3 Are the farms growing peas a long way from, or close to the factory?

One step further

1 As well as frozen in what other ways can you buy peas?

2 **Talking point:** Does the food you eat matter?

Talk about what foods you think are good, or bad for you. This chart shows what the experts say.

Copy the chart and put a tick if you agree, or a cross if you disagree.

FOOD GOOD FOR YOU	✓ or X	FOOD BAD FOR YOU	✓ or X
Wholemeal bread		Sugar	
Fresh fruit		Sweets	
Fresh vegetables		Fat and things fried in fat	
Lean Meat		Salt	
Fish		Cakes	

Find out why foods like sweets are bad for you.

POTATO CRISPS

MONDAY   TUESDAY   WEDNESDAY

There is no rush to get potatoes to the factory. They do not lose their fresh taste as quickly as peas. A special variety of potato called **Record** is grown. Record is a hard potato and makes a pale coloured crisp.

This diagram shows what happens to the potatoes in the factory:

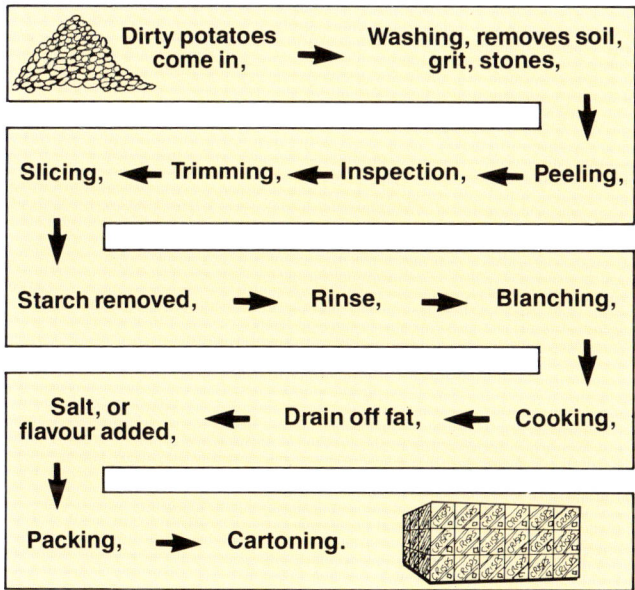

GOODS OUT — GUDSPUD CRISPS

New Potatoes · INSTANT MASH · STARCH

Potato RINGS · Ready-Cut FROZEN CHIPS

Dirty potatoes come in, → Washing, removes soil, grit, stones,

Slicing, ← Trimming, ← Inspection, ← Peeling,

Starch removed, → Rinse, → Blanching,

Salt, or flavour added, ← Drain off fat, ← Cooking,

Packing, → Cartoning.

Assignment

1 Why must the variety of potato be hard? (Think how thin the slices have to be)

2 1000 kilos of potatoes make about 300 kilos of crisps. How many kilos are 'lost'?

3 Write two ways some potato is 'lost' in making crisps. (Remember potatoes are partly made of water.)

One step further

1 Make a class survey of favourite crisp flavours. Draw a graph of your results.

2 Make a list of the things potatoes can be made into. Look at the pictures for clues.

3 Why do many people prefer to buy processed potatoes rather than fresh ones?

AT THE SEASIDE

Alnmouth is a small village on the North Sea coast. It is a quiet place with a few guest houses. It is a long way from any large towns.

Blackpool is close to many large towns. More holiday-makers visit Blackpool than any other seaside place. It has many hotels, guest-houses, theatres and fun parks.

Assignment A

1 Which would you prefer to visit? Give your reasons why.

2 Why do more people visit Blackpool than Alnmouth?

3 Which is best for the following activities? Copy and complete the chart.

The best place for	Alnmouth	Blackpool
quiet walking holiday		
playing bingo		
going to the theatre		
bird watching		
fun at an amusement park		
walking along a pier		
farm visits		

Some beaches are covered by sand, rocks, pebbles or mud. Stones, sand and mud are washed along the coast by the sea to make beaches.

Photo A

Assignment B

Look at photo A.

1 What kind of beach is shown?

2 List six things you can see people doing.

3 Imagine you are someone in the photo. Write a postcard to a friend about your holiday.

4 What kind of beach do you like best? Why?

One step further

Pollution is a problem on many beaches.

1 What are the children on this beach doing?

2 How do you think beaches and sea water become polluted?

Write your own beach code.

Do	Don't

ISLE OF WIGHT

Photo A   The Needles

Photo B   Sandown

1 Why are the rocks in photo A called the Needles?

2 What is the building on the Needles? Why is it there?

3 Why are there no buildings by the beach at the Needles?

4 Look at photo B. Give two reasons why Sandown looks a good place for a holiday.

5 What kind of beach does it have?

6 Is Sandown on high or low land?

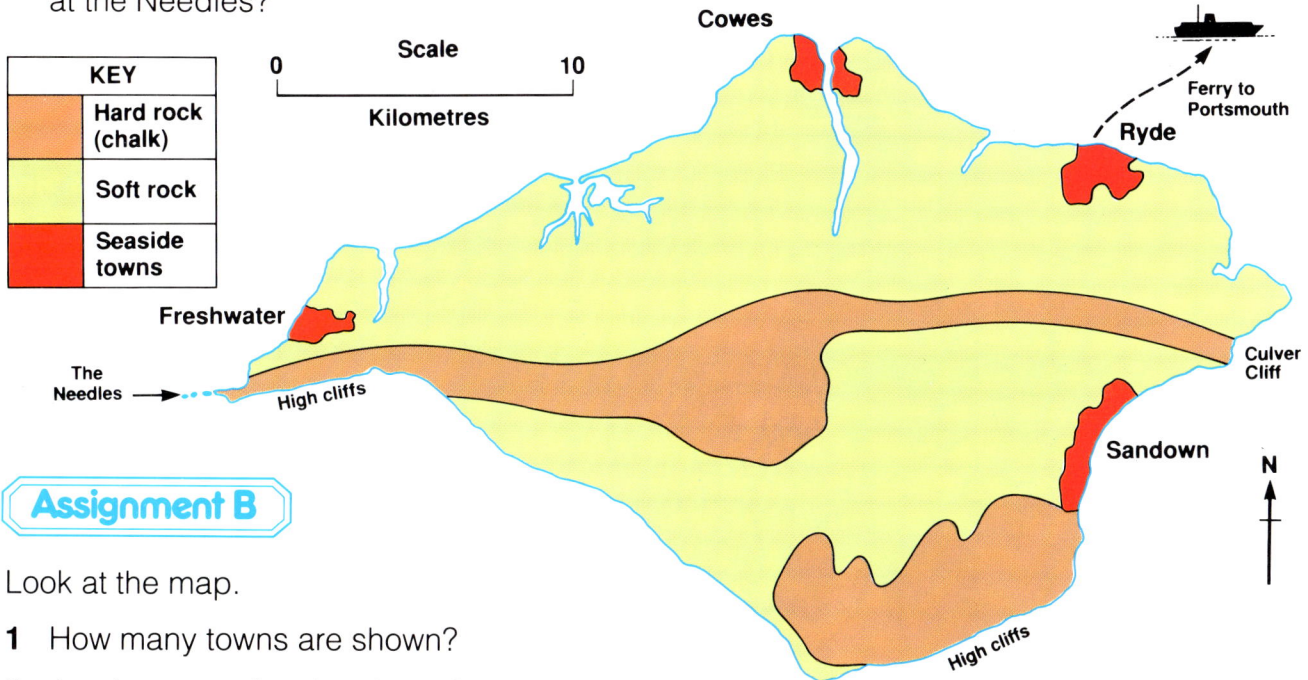

KEY	
	Hard rock (chalk)
	Soft rock
	Seaside towns

Scale 0 — 10 Kilometres

Cowes

Ferry to Portsmouth

Ryde

Freshwater

Culver Cliff

The Needles →

High cliffs

Sandown

N

High cliffs

Assignment B

Look at the map.

1 How many towns are shown?

2 Are they on soft or hard rock?

3 Are the high cliffs made of soft or hard rock?

4 Which direction does the ferry take to Portsmouth?

5 Are the Needles in the north, south, east or west of the island?

One step further

1 Compare the coasts in the two photographs.

2 A boat is shipwrecked on the Needles. Imagine you are the pilot of the rescue helicopter. Describe what happens.

Sea waves are strong. They crash into the land and quickly wear away the soft rock. Even hard rocks have cracks in them. The sea's waves widen the cracks into caves. Rocks above the caves fall into the sea. Slowly little islands are formed. The Needles were formed in this way.

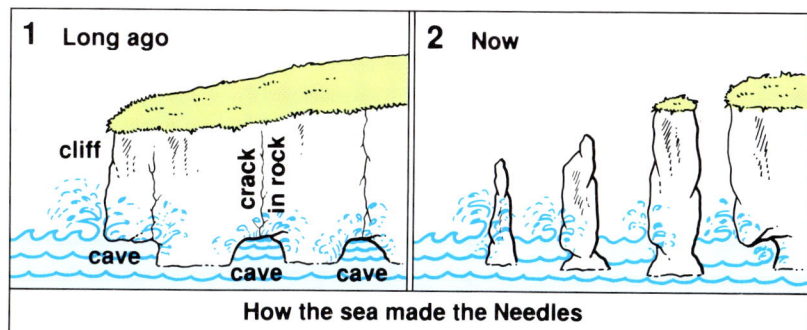

1 Long ago

cliff

crack in rock

cave

cave   cave

2 Now

How the sea made the Needles

MOVING HOUSE

Mrs Johnson is going to have a baby.

I can't wait to have our own garden to play in!

I'm not sure that I want to move. There will be no backyard wall to score goals against.

There'll be trees and a garage to play in....!

I'll never find any friends and I don't want to move school.

Aren't you fed up of sharing with ME!

It would be GREAT not sharing again!

PRIVATE DAVID'S ROOM KEEP OUT

Assignment

1 Why does Sally want to move?

2 Why is David not so sure about moving?

3 What will the new house have that the old house has not?

4 Here is a chart which shows how many houses Sally, David and some of their friends have lived in.

Number of homes		
1	2	3
	Ben	
Teresa	Sally	
Ivor	David	Emma

Now do these.

   a) Who has lived in the most houses?

   b) Which girl has moved twice?

5 Ask 5 children in your class how many homes they have lived in since they were born. Draw your own block graph to show the results.

One step further

1 Copy and complete the 'who thinks what' chart.

Reason for move	Parents	Children
More space	✓	✓
Garage		
Garden to play in		
Own bedrooms		
Quiet road		

2 If you were told you were moving house tomorrow what would you miss the most?

3 Make a survey of three adults (teachers, parents, relatives or friends) to find out how many times they have moved house.

4 Imagine you are a furniture remover. Write a story about the difficulties of your job. Here are some words to help you: *Heavy piano, tall wardrobe, steep stairs, narrow doors, raining.*

CHOOSING A HOME

The Johnson family are looking for a new house. The estate agent is showing them pictures and plans of four new houses.

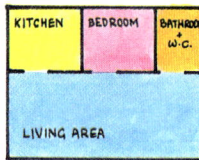

Can it have a play area -- so we can play football?

It must have at least three bedrooms---

What sort of house are you looking for?

And it must be fairly cheap and near a shop.

Can it be near my school and have a garden to play in?

B. Detached bungalow

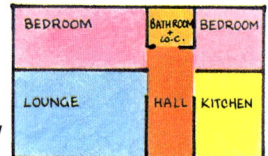

BEDROOM	BATHROOM w.c.	BEDROOM
LOUNGE	HALL	KITCHEN

KITCHEN	BEDROOM	BATHROOM w.c.
LIVING AREA		

A. Small flat

A Small flat: medium price

B Detached bungalow: medium price

Assignment A

1 Is home **A** suitable for the Johnsons?

2 Give 3 reasons for your answer to question 1.

3 How many flats can you see in picture **A**?

4 If you lived in one of the flats shown in picture **A**, on which floor would you choose to live?

   a) The ground floor
   b) The first floor
   c) The second floor

5 Write about why you would make this choice.

6 If you were an old age pensioner which floor might be best for you?

   Give reasons.

7 How many of the homes are detached?

BEDROOM | BATHROOM + W.C. | BEDROOM

BEDROOM | BEDROOM

STAIRS

SHOWER ROOM

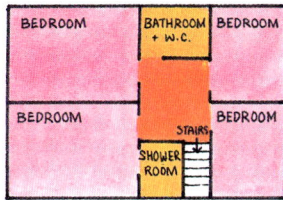

PLAN OF UPSTAIRS

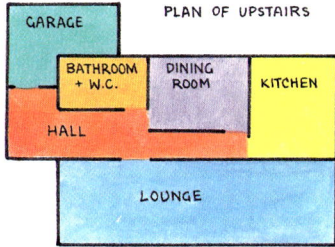

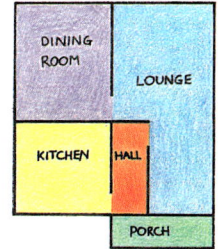

GARAGE

BATHROOM + W.C. | DINING ROOM | KITCHEN

HALL

LOUNGE

PLAN OF DOWNSTAIRS

C. Detached house

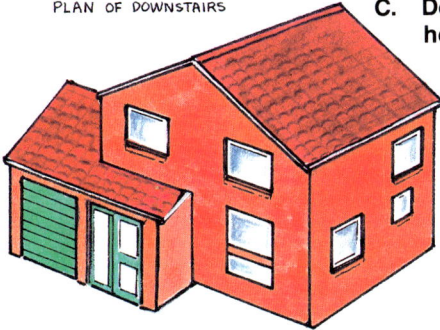

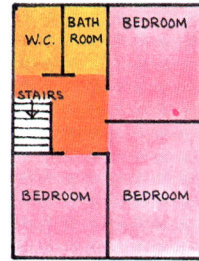

Which house did they choose?

D Semi-detached house

W.C. | BATH ROOM | BEDROOM

STAIRS

BEDROOM | BEDROOM

PLAN OF UPSTAIRS

DINING ROOM | LOUNGE

KITCHEN | HALL

PORCH

PLAN OF DOWNSTAIRS
PLAN OF DOWNSTAIRS

C   Detached house: high price

D   Semi-detached house: medium price

Assignment B

1   The Johnsons have made a chart which helps them compare the four types of homes.

Complete the chart by looking at the plans.

One section has been done for you.

2   Which house do you think the Johnsons chose?
Give your reasons.

3   Which is the biggest house **A**, **B**, **C** or **D**?

One step further

1   Draw a picture and a plan of your own home.

2   Describe the sort of house you would really like to live in.

Room	Home A	Home B	Home C	Home D
Lounge	yes			
Dining Room	no			
Kitchen	yes			
Number of Bedrooms	1			
Bathroom	yes			
Toilet	yes			
Shower Room	no			
Hall	no			
Total number of rooms	4			
medium price (m) high price (h)	m			

CHOOSING A HOME

Dr and Mrs Dover and Eileen and Ben

P.C. Clew

Mr and Mrs Singh

Mrs Dale

Mrs Bell and Ivor

Mr and Mrs Green and Teresa

When a family becomes larger or smaller they may look for a new home. If P.C. Clew gets married and has children his flat will be too small. They might move into house **B** or **C**.

One step further A

Family	Present Home	Future Home	Reason
P.C. Clew	A	B or C	Bigger family
Mrs Dale			
Mr and Mrs Singh			
Dr and Mrs Dover, Eileen & Ben			
Mrs Bell and Ivor			
Mr and Mrs Green and Teresa			

Assignment A

These people need homes. Look at pages 54 and 55. Which home is most suitable for each family?

Copy this chart and put in your answers.

Home A	Home B	Home C	Home D
			Johnsons

Copy this chart and record the changes that might happen if...

Mrs Dale's grandson comes to live with her.

Mr & Mrs Singh have two children.

Mrs Bell gets married again. Her new husband, Mr Down, has a son, Neil.

Eileen and Ben grow up and leave home.

Mr & Mrs Green are divorced. Teresa lives with Mr Green. Mrs Green is left on her own.

People usually move to different homes at different times in their lives. This is the life of Diana.

Diana is seven.

Diana is 23.

Diana is 34 and has a family.

Diana is 56. Her children have grown up and left home.

Diana is 77. She is a widow and lives on her own.

Here are the five homes in which Diana lived.

Two bedroom bungalow.

One bedroom home.

A warden lives near to look after old people.

One bedroomed flat.

Three bedroom terraced house.

Assignment B

Copy the table and choose a home for Diana at the 5 different ages.

DIANA'S AGE	WHO IS LIVING WITH DIANA	WHICH HOME
1. Seven	mum and dad	
2.		
3.		
4.		
5.		

Three bedroom semi-detached house.

One step further B

Find out how many different homes these people have lived in:

Your teacher. The caretaker or cook. Your Mum or Dad. Your Grandma or Grandad.

Oblique view of the estate

This is the estate where the Johnsons are buying a house. The helicopter pilot gets a slanting view of the area in front of him. We call this an **oblique** view.

Now look at the plan of the same estate on the next page. The plan shows everything from directly above.

We call this a **plan** view.

Assignment A

1 Which view shows how tall the houses are - the oblique or plan view?

2 On the oblique view, which looks bigger, the front or back garden of bungalow 4?

3 On the plan view, which looks bigger, the front or back garden of bungalow 4?

4 Look at the oblique view and name three things that move. Why are these not shown on plans?

5 Name two places where it would be dangerous to play. Say why these two places are dangerous.

One step further A

1 Draw a sketch map of the area around your home.

   Show on it - your home, your friends' homes, the street names and where you play.

   Give the map a key.

2 Write a story about a girl or boy living at 5, Oak Close and where they play out of doors.

KEY

⊞	Flats
▫	Bungalow
⌐	Detached house
⊓	Semi-detached house
▮	Main road
▮	Side road
▮	Footpath
▬	Railway
⧟	Bridge
⊞	Rumble strip
•	Children's play area
▮	Waste ground
🌳	Woods
▮	Grassfields
▮	River and pool of water

SCALE

0 10 20 30 40 50 60 70 80 90 100 METRES

N
W — E
S

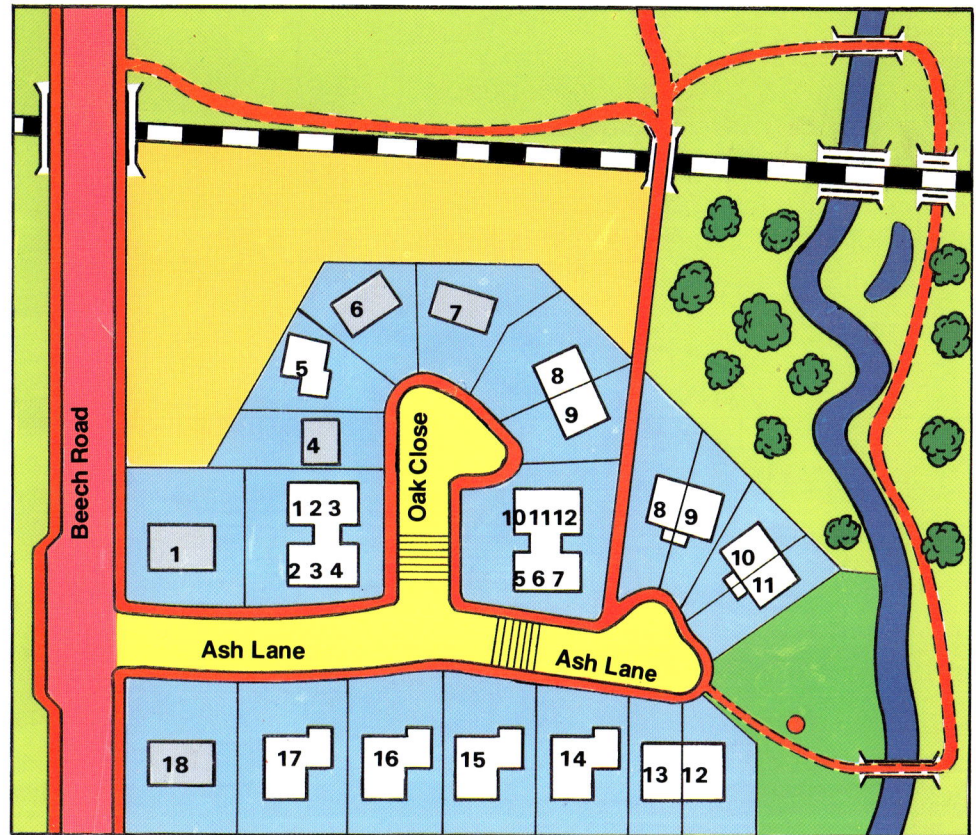

Map showing Beech Road, Oak Close, Ash Lane with numbered houses.

Assignment B

1 The symbol ///// is found along Oak Close and Ash Lane. What do you think it shows? Use the oblique picture to help you.

2 Which is the road that has the most detached houses along it?

3 What is a rumble strip? Why is it in Ash Lane and Oak Close?

4 How many bridges are there on the map?

5 The Johnsons have never had a garden before. They want a back garden that faces South so that it will get plenty of sunshine. Choose a semi-detached house that will suit them.

One step further B

The Dover family have moved into Number 5 Oak Close.

Describe a walk they could make using roads and footpaths.

Say when they are walking South, East and so on.

Explain what they would see on their walk in the correct order starting and finishing at Oak Close.

Rumble strip

People move homes for many reasons. Some people move only a few kilometres. Others travel halfway around the world. Many people move to find work, others to escape danger.

The factories in my home town closed down so I came here to look for work.

John Minor

My grandparents escaped from Uganda. All the Asians had to leave in 1972.

Nita Patel

I am Jewish. I fled from Germany in the 1930s.

Mrs Fischer

I came from Barbados to work as a nurse.

Ann Roberts

My mum came from Hungary in 1956 when the Russians attacked.

Marela Conway

Britain was short of factory workers when I came in 1960 to find work.

Mr Hussein

I moved here from Australia to study at the local College.

Bob Down

The map on page 61 shows the nine countries where the people or their families moved from.

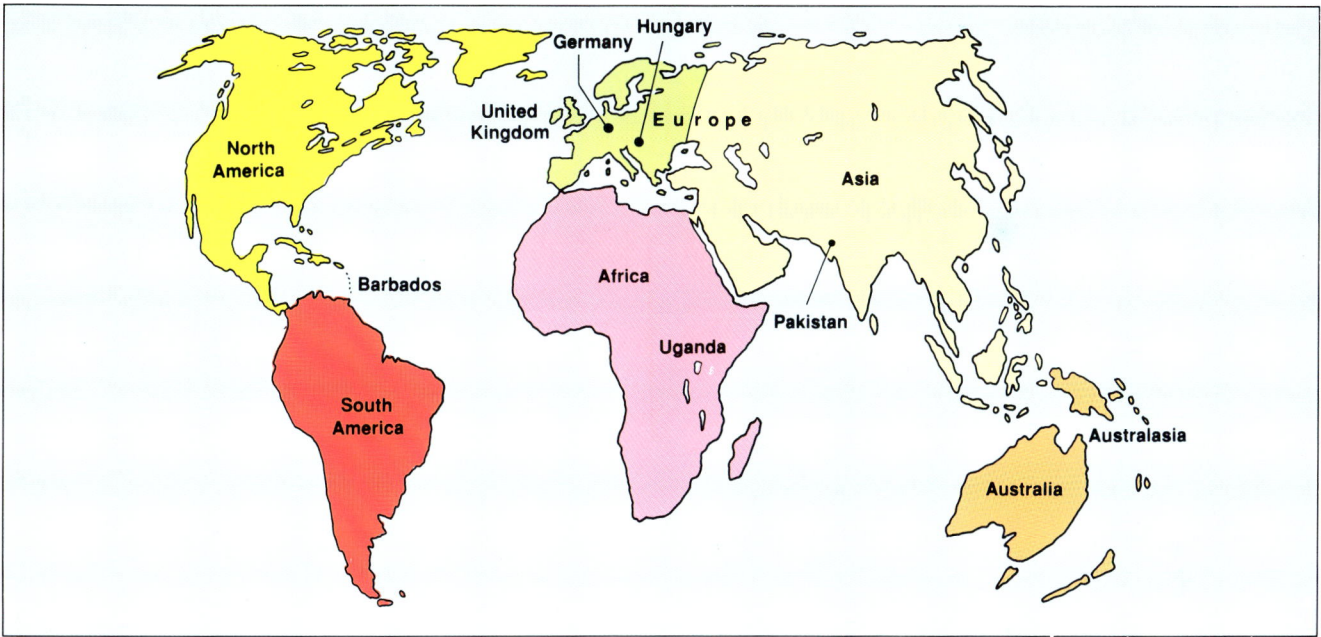

Assignment A

1 Copy and complete the chart. The first one has been done for you.

Person/Family	From	Continent	Work	Study	Danger
John Minor	United Kingdom	Europe	✔		
Nita Patel					

2 On a copy of a blank world map write the name of each person on the country she/he (or the family) came from.

3 Draw lines joining each country to the United Kingdom.

4 Who travelled the shortest distance? Who travelled the longest distance?

Ms Scot

Mr Bolton

Ms French

Ms London

Mr Ireland

Long ago in Britain, when people moved from one town to another they were often given the name of the town they had left. So if two Johns arrived in Stoke, one from Bolton and one from London they would become known as John Bolton and John London.

One step further

1 Find on a map of the British Isles the places these five people's ancestors came from long ago.

2 Make a list of six people who have place names for their last names.

3 Find those places on a map.

4 Only men's and single women's names give us clues to their ancestors. Why?

THE WORLD

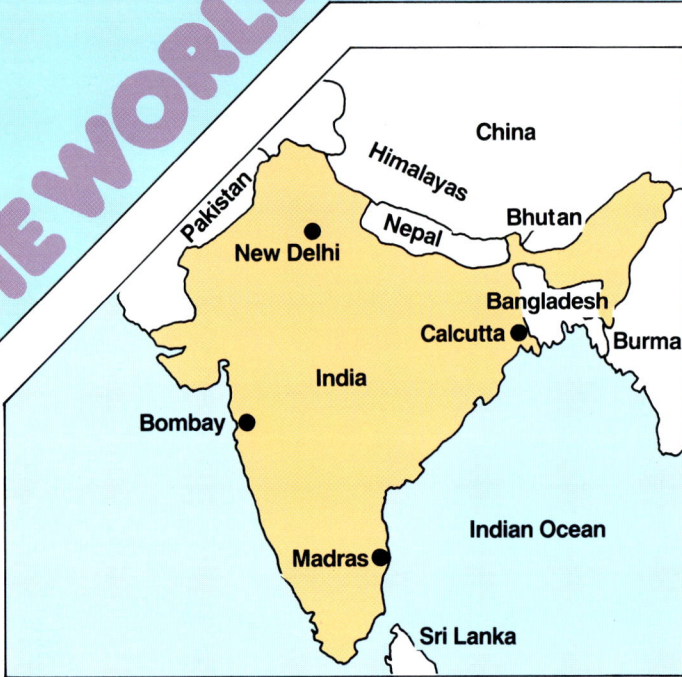

Map of India and its neighbours

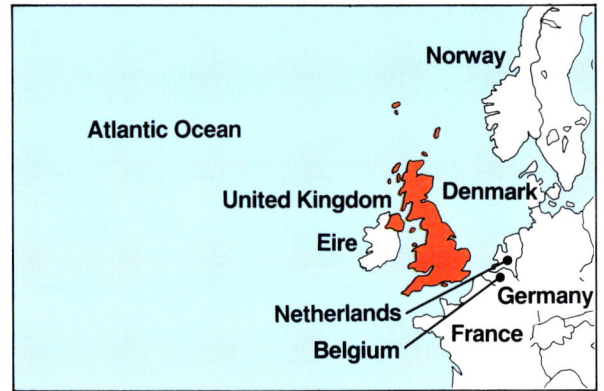

China

Pakistan

Himalayas

Nepal

Bhutan

New Delhi

Bangladesh

Calcutta

Burma

India

Bombay

Indian Ocean

Madras

Sri Lanka

Map of India and its neighbours.

Map of the United Kingdom

Norway

Atlantic Ocean

United Kingdom

Denmark

Eire

Germany

Netherlands

France

Belgium

Map of the United Kingdom and countries close to it.

0   400   800   1200   1600   2000 Kilometres

(Scale: one centimetre on each map represents 400 kilometres.)

The scale is the same for all three maps. One centimetre on the map represents 400 kilometres on the ground.

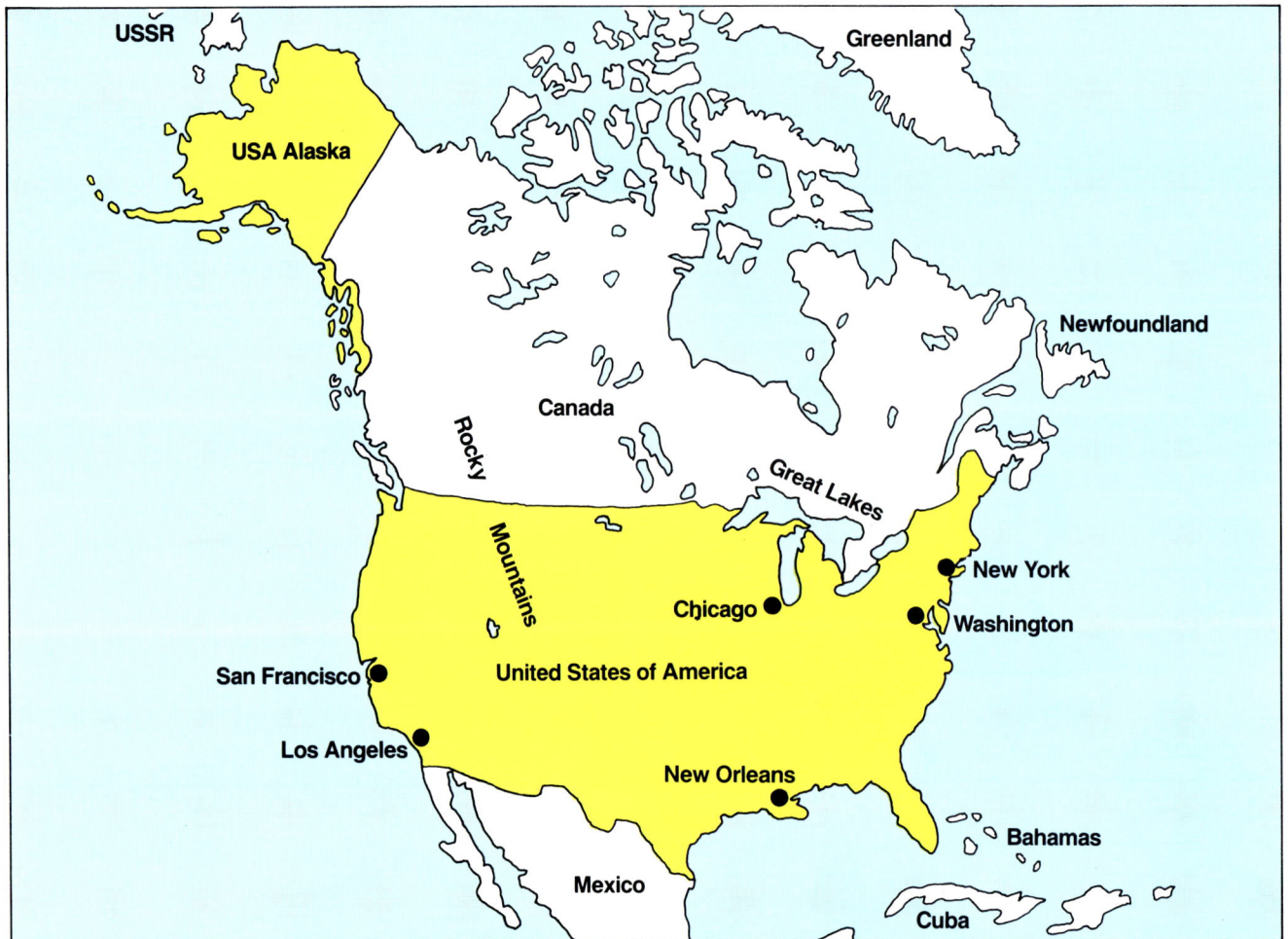

Map of the United States of America

USSR

Greenland

USA Alaska

Newfoundland

Canada

Rocky

Great Lakes

Mountains

New York

Chicago

Washington

San Francisco

United States of America

Los Angeles

New Orleans

Bahamas

Mexico

Cuba

Map of the United States of America and its neighbours.

The world has seven large land areas. These are called **continents**. The seven continents are shown on this map, in different colours. The large water areas, called **oceans**, are shown in blue. About three-quarters of the surface of the world is covered by water.

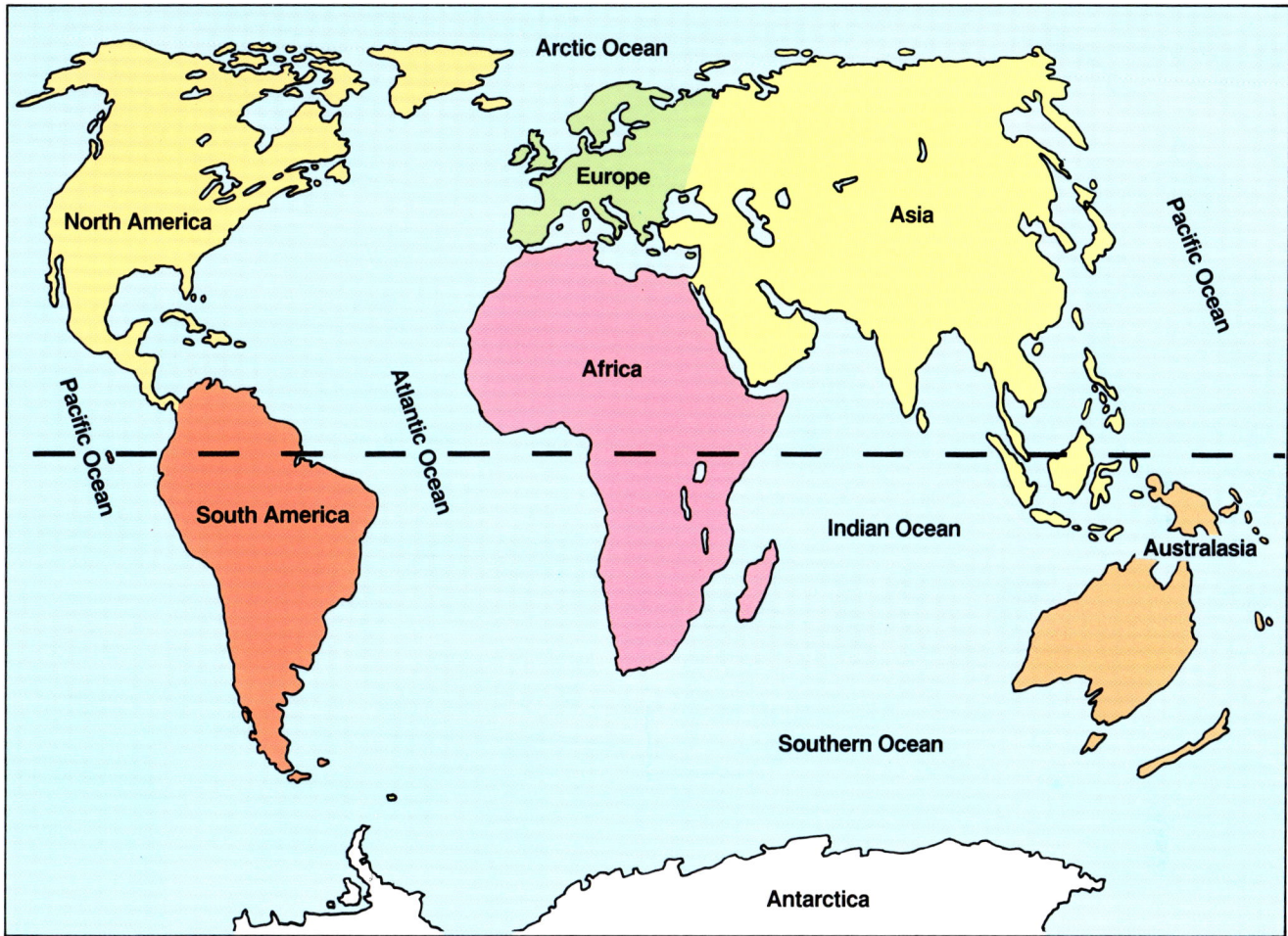

Arctic Ocean

Europe

Asia

North America

Pacific Ocean

Africa

Atlantic Ocean

Pacific Ocean

Indian Ocean

South America

Australasia

Southern Ocean

Antarctica

Assignment A

1 Which is the largest of the three countries, India, U.K., or U.S.A.?

2 Which is the smallest of the three countries, India, U.K., or U.S.A.?

3 Copy this table and show the 'neighbours':

Country	Name three countries close by		
India			
U.S.A.			
U.K.			

Assignment B

1 Which is the biggest continent?

2 Which are the two smallest continents? (Antartica is the 5th largest)

3 Name three large oceans.

4 Copy and complete this table:

Country	Continent
1. India	
2. U.S.A.	
3. U.K.	

SHOPPING GAME

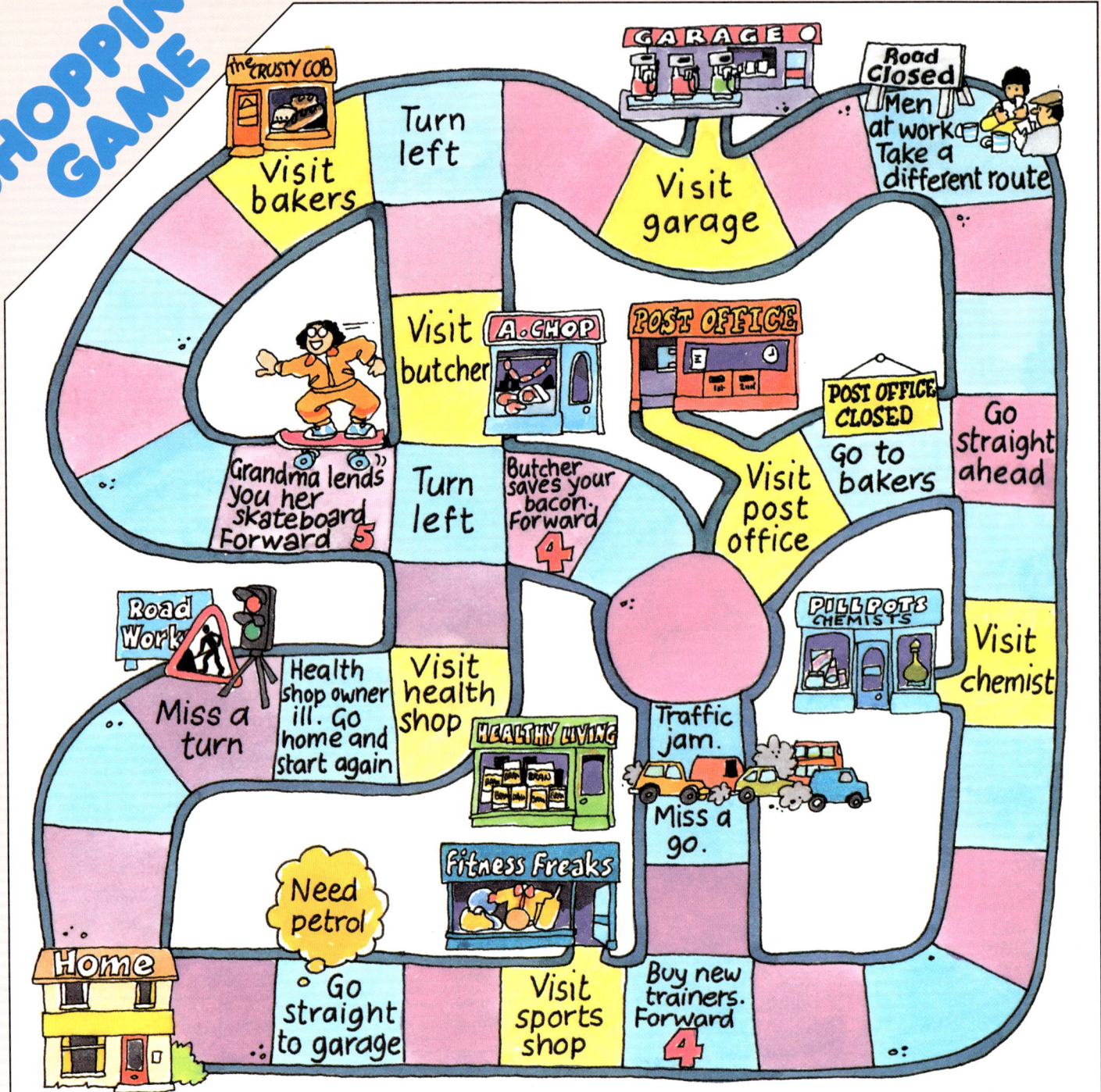

the CRUSTY COB

Visit bakers

Turn left

GARAGE

Visit garage

Road Closed

Men at work Take a different route

Visit butcher

A. CHOP

POST OFFICE

POST OFFICE CLOSED

Go to bakers

Go straight ahead

Grandma lends you her skateboard Forward 5

Turn left

Butcher saves your bacon. Forward 4

Visit post office

PILL POTS CHEMISTS

Visit chemist

Road Works

Miss a turn

Health shop owner ill. Go home and start again

Visit health shop

HEALTHY LIVING

Traffic jam. Miss a go.

Need petrol

Fitness Freaks

Home

Go straight to garage

Visit sports shop

Buy new trainers. Forward 4

Going shopping

You need

a die   counters   a friend

How to play

Start from home. Each player has a shopping list. The winner is the first to collect all the shopping and return home.

Shopping list 1
bacon
football boots
health food
medicine
bread
stamps

Player 1

Shopping list 2
trainers
petrol
sausages
shampoo
birthday cake
birthday card

Player 2